IOSOP
Culture

SECONDARY
CLASSROOM EDITION

For information about school-wide professional development, team training, or individual coaching in the application of Loving our Students on Purpose please contact:

- www.godwinconsulting.com.au
- admin@godwinconsulting.com.au

Editor: Allison Slack
Cover Design by Ashley Beck
Interior Design and Layout by Daniel Morales
ISBN: 978-0-6459046-5-9

DEDICATION

This book is dedicated to Kings Christian College whose leadership and community have embraced Loving Our Students on Purpose and embedded its principles into their culture. Your commitment to connection, joy, and responsibility stands as an inspiration to others.

Books

Loving our Students on Purpose
Cultural Architect (coming 2026)

LoSoP Momentum Series

(Weekly aligned foundational philosophy of Loving our Students on Purpose)
Staffroom Edition––book, ebook, or video series available
Future editions coming soon!

LoSoP Culture Series

(Weekly aligned foundational values to build a Culture of Love)
Boardroom Edition
Staffroom Edition
Primary Classroom Edition
Secondary Classroom Edition
Family Room Edition

Podcasts

Loving Our Students on Purpose Journey Podcast
Culture Daily: Education Edition

Resources Available

www.godwinconsulting.com.au
Explore our full range of LoSoP resources designed to bring
connection and joyful responsibility into everyday practice
—from Desk Flips, Printable Poster Collections, and Flash Cards
to Online Courses, Bookmarks, and more.

For bulk purchases email admin@godwinconsulting.com.au

TABLE OF CONTENTS

BUILDING A CULTURE OF LOVE

Welcome to the LoSoP Culture Series: Classroom Edition

Creating Classrooms Where Every Student Feels Beloved,
Chosen, and Cherished

This series is your invitation to create something lasting in your classroom: a culture of love where every student feels beloved, chosen, and cherished. Whether you teach in a primary or secondary setting, this resource will help your class grow together in respect, responsibility, and relationships that last.

The *LoSoP Culture Series* is built on a simple but powerful truth: love changes everything. I don't mean the fluffy or feel-good kind of love, but the kind of love that shows up with boundaries, grace, and purpose––the kind of love that holds space for challenge, speaks the truth kindly, and helps students learn how to restore connection when things go wrong.

Across 40 weekly sessions, your class will explore the building blocks of a strong, connected culture. Each week focuses on a key principle of connection, drawn from four foundational pillars: *Healthy Relationships, Joyful Responsibility, Genuine Restoration,* and *Leadership Development.*

This series has been created to align with the same weekly focus used in boardrooms, staff meetings, family homes, and classrooms. That means your students will be learning the same values that are being lived out by their teachers, families, and leaders—building a shared language of love and connection across every part of their world.

What Is a Culture of Love?

A culture of love doesn't happen by accident—it's created on purpose. It's formed in the way we speak to each other, how we handle mistakes, how we set boundaries, and how we build trust through everyday moments.

This series is guided by four core truths:

1. Our goal is connection.
2. Love is a powerful choice.
3. Fear is the enemy of connection.
4. Building and protecting connection is a learning journey.

You'll return to these truths again and again as your class grows together through weekly conversations and shared practice.

The Four Pillars of a Classroom Culture of Love

Each week, you and your students will explore one or more of the four culture-building pillars:

- Healthy Relationships––where every student feels safe, valued, and included
- Joyful Responsibility––where students learn to own their actions and support their peers

- Genuine Restoration--where students practise repairing trust and reconnecting after mistakes
- Leadership Development--where students grow in confidence, courage, and positive influence

These pillars will help you create a classroom where connection is normal, not rare—and where students learn how to build community, not just follow rules.

How to Use This Series

Each session includes a core idea, simple language that's age-appropriate, space for discussion, and a weekly practice. It's designed to be flexible—you can use it in morning circles, well-being blocks, class meetings, or homeroom time. It works with whole classes or small groups, and can be adapted to suit the needs of your students.

You don't need to have all the answers—you just need to be willing to grow together.

Why It Matters

In classrooms where love leads, students thrive. They take more risks, recover from setbacks, and learn how to take care of themselves and others. They grow not just in academics, but in character, resilience, and compassion.

This series will help you create the kind of classroom where connection comes first—and everything else follows.

This is a classroom built on love—on purpose.

A NOTE FROM BERNII

Dear Educator,

Welcome to the *LoSoP Culture Series: Classroom Edition*—a resource created to support you in building a classroom where connection is the foundation, not the reward.

Teaching has always been about more than content. It's about relationships—the small, powerful moments that shape how students see themselves, each other, and the world around them. It's in your tone of voice, your body language, your ability to hold boundaries with kindness, and your commitment to repair when things go wrong.

This series is here to walk alongside you as you lead a culture of love in your classroom—one conversation at a time. Each week, you and your students will reflect on ideas that matter: how we treat people, how we take responsibility, how we repair trust, and how we grow as leaders together.

These are not just classroom management tools. They are life skills. And every time you model them, you're helping students build internal muscles for empathy, resilience, and self-awareness.

You won't need to have all the answers. You won't need to get it perfect. But your willingness to lead with love—to invite your students into real conversations, and to keep showing up with grace and courage—is enough to create something extraordinary.

Thank you for being the kind of teacher who chooses connection over control, courage over comfort, and restoration over reaction. Your students may not always have the words to say it, but the culture you create is shaping who they're becoming—and they will carry that with them long after they leave your classroom.

I'm cheering you on every step of the way.

Keep choosing connection,
Bernii

HOW TO USE THE LOSOP CULTURE SERIES: SECONDARY CLASSROOM EDITION

Creating Classrooms Where Every Student Feels Beloved, Chosen, and Cherished

The *LoSoP Culture Series: Secondary Classroom Edition* is a practical, flexible resource designed to help students build meaningful relationships, take ownership of their actions, restore trust when it's broken, and grow as young leaders.

Each week, you'll engage in a short session that introduces a key concept and invites real conversations about how we treat one another, how we lead ourselves, and how we contribute to a culture of love in our school.

How to Get Started

1. **Weekly Sessions**

   Each session follows a consistent structure that helps students engage with the content and apply it to real life. The format is designed to feel familiar each week, thus building rhythm, trust, and impact over time:

- **Learn**--Start with the main idea for the week, using relatable examples to make the concept accessible and relevant.

- **Let's Make It Real**--Explore the idea through a metaphor, short story, or personal reflection. This helps anchor the lesson emotionally and practically.

- **Discuss**--Lead a class discussion that invites open conversation, shared insights, and respectful reflection. This is where connection grows and perspectives expand.

- **Connect**--Students meet in Connect Groups (up to five students) to reflect more deeply. Each group selects a leader for the week to help guide the discussion.

  - The Connect Leader reads one question at a time, makes sure everyone has a chance to speak, and helps the group move through all four questions.

  - These conversations build empathy, strengthen peer relationships, and give students space to practise honest, respectful dialogue.

- **Do**--Each week includes a challenge or practical action step to help students apply the concept in their everyday life.

- **End-of-Week Reflection**--Use the final reflection questions to check in, notice growth, and consider what's next. These conversations promote accountability and shared learning.

2. **Flexible Timing**
   The sessions are designed to fit within short, intentional moments in your week:

- Use them during well-being time, morning check-ins, or homeroom.

- Fit them into a class meeting or leadership session.
- Adjust the timing to suit your group—some discussions will be quick, others may go deeper.

3. **Adapt for Your Students**
   Every class is different, and this series is designed to be flexible:

- Use more visual prompts and concrete examples for younger or less experienced groups.
- For older students, encourage deeper thinking, independent reflection, and leadership in Connect Groups.
- Try partner chats, small groups, or whole-class discussions depending on your classroom culture.

4. **Create a Safe Space for Sharing**
   Before each session, revisit your class agreement or group expectations.

- Remind students that every voice matters, and everyone deserves to be heard without judgment.
- Let students help set expectations around how they'll speak, listen, and protect each other's emotional safety.
- As the teacher, model openness by sharing your own reflections—showing students that personal growth is something we all do together.

5. **Track Growth**
   Encourage students to reflect on their progress week by week:

- Use the End-of-Week Reflection to help them notice when they applied what they learned.

- Provide space for journaling, drawing, or goal-setting in response to the sessions.
- Support students to track their growth as part of their leadership or well-being portfolios.

6. **Integrate with Your Curriculum**

   This series aligns with key learning areas like:

- Social-emotional learning and health
- English and literacy (through writing, speaking, and reflection)
- Leadership and personal development programs

Weave weekly themes into your lessons through related literature, current events, group work, or behaviour conversations.

7. **Celebrate Progress**

   Notice and name when students practise the principles they've learned:

- Acknowledge moments of kindness, responsibility, or repair.
- Highlight strong leadership and courageous choices.
- Consider creating a class reflection wall or digital journal where students can share what they're proud of.

Celebrating growth builds momentum—and makes values visible.

8. **8. Revisit and Reinforce**

   Some lessons will hit home right away. Others may take time or need repetition.

- Feel free to revisit topics when challenges arise.
- Reinforce the key ideas in your day-to-day teaching, class routines, and behaviour responses.

This isn't about getting it perfect—it's about growing stronger, together.

Final Thoughts

This series is more than a collection of lessons—it's a journey into what it means to create a classroom culture built on connection, responsibility, restoration, and leadership.

When we give students space to be heard, supported, and empowered, we shape more than a positive learning environment—we shape the kind of people they're becoming.

Thank you for leading this journey with your students. The culture you're building will shape their lives far beyond the classroom.

TOP TIP

GET READY WITH A FEELINGS WHEEL

Before you begin the *LoSoP Culture* Series with your students, we recommend printing a large feelings wheel poster and displaying it in your classroom. You can find a variety of feelings wheels online by simply googling "Feelings Wheel"— choose one that suits the age group you're working with.

A number of topics in this series include a "How do you feel?" question. It's important to focus on the student's own experience, rather than asking, "How did that make you feel?" which can unintentionally place the responsibility for feelings outside the student. By asking "How do you feel?", we support students to take ownership of their internal emotional experiences.

Encourage students to move beyond basic labels like *sad, bad, mad,* or *glad,* and instead explore the feelings wheel to identify a more specific emotion. This simple practice helps expand their emotional vocabulary and builds their capacity to express themselves with clarity and confidence--an essential skill for connection, empathy, and self-awareness.

All emotions are good. They exist to signal that action is needed. Sometimes emotions reveal that a boundary has been crossed and invite us to take responsibility for how we protect our future boundaries. At other times they highlight a need that requires attention, or they expose a fear that has been triggered. Emotions can also be a signal that something deserves to be celebrated. Whatever the emotion, it is doing its job of communicating. Our task — and the task we teach our students — is to listen well and respond with wisdom.

PART ONE

CULTIVATING HEALTHY RELATIONSHIPS

In this section, students will learn how to build strong and meaningful connections with the people around them—classmates, teachers, friends, and family. Together, we'll explore what it means to communicate well, show empathy, build trust, and treat others with genuine respect.

Rather than just talking about relationships, students will have the chance to practise these skills in real-life ways—through stories, chats, and everyday situations. They'll begin to see that healthy relationships don't just happen—they grow when we choose to be kind, listen well, and look out for each other.

The goal? To help every student feel more confident in how they connect with others and to create a classroom culture where respect, understanding, and compassion are a natural part of daily life.

WEEK 1:

THE POWER OF LISTENING

*"Listening is not a skill; it's a discipline. Anybody can do it.
All you have to do is keep your mouth shut."*
—Peter Drucker

Learn:

Listening is one of the most powerful ways to show respect and build strong relationships. When we truly listen to others, we make them feel heard, valued, and understood. It's easy to interrupt or think about what we're going to say next, but real listening involves focusing on the person speaking and taking in what they're saying. Good listeners are trusted more and have better relationships because they show that they care.

Consider:

In a classroom discussion, one student interrupts others and quickly gives their opinion, while another listens quietly until the speaker finishes before responding. The students who are listened to feel respected and valued, while those who are interrupted feel ignored. The listener builds stronger relationships because they take the time to understand others.

Let's Make It Real:

Invite students to talk to the person next to them about a time when they felt truly listened to by someone. How did it make them feel? Share how being a good listener has helped in their friendships or family life.

Discuss:

- Why is it important to listen carefully when others are speaking?
- Can you think of a time when not listening caused a misunderstanding or problem?
- What can you do to become a better listener this week?

Connect:

- How do you think you're going with this skill in your own life?
- If you had to give yourself a score out of 10 (10 being awesome), what would you give yourself?
- Can you think of someone who's really good at this? What do they do that stands out to you?
- What's one small thing you can try this week to bump your score up by one point?

Do:

This week, practice being a good listener. Focus on what the other person is saying without interrupting or thinking about your reply. Show that you're listening by asking questions or summarising what they said. Notice how listening strengthens your relationships.

End-of-Week Reflection:

- How did you practice active listening this week?
- Can you think of a time this week when listening carefully changed how a situation turned out?
- What did you learn about the power of listening in building better relationships?

WEEK 2:

GIVING AND RECEIVING FEEDBACK

"Feedback is the breakfast of champions."
—Rick Tate

Learn:

Feedback is an important tool for growth and improvement. It helps us understand how we are doing and what we can work on. Giving feedback means offering helpful, kind, and constructive advice to others, while receiving feedback means being open to learning from others' observations. Feedback isn't about criticism—it's about learning and making positive changes. When we embrace feedback, we improve and help others improve as well.

Consider:

During a class project, one student offers feedback to their partner on how to improve their presentation. Instead of feeling upset, the partner listens and makes adjustments. As a result, the presentation is stronger, and both students feel proud of their work. By giving and receiving feedback respectfully, they help each other succeed.

Let's Make It Real:

Invite students to talk to the person next to them about a time when they gave or received feedback. How did the feedback help them improve, and how did they feel about it?

Discuss:

- Why is it important to be open to feedback, even if it's about something we need to improve?
- Can you think of a time when giving or receiving feedback helped you or someone else grow?
- What is one way you can give helpful feedback to someone in a kind and respectful way?

Connect:

- How do you think you're going with this skill in your own life?
- If you had to give yourself a score out of 10 (10 being awesome), what would you give yourself?
- Can you think of someone who's really good at this? What do they do that stands out to you?
- What's one small thing you can try this week to bump your score up by one point?

Do:

This week, practice giving and receiving feedback. If you need to offer feedback, do it kindly and constructively. If you receive feedback, listen with an open mind and use it to improve. Notice how feedback helps you and others grow.

End-of-Week Reflection:

- How did you give or receive feedback this week?
- How did that feedback help you or someone else improve?
- What did you learn about the importance of constructive feedback?

WEEK 3:

THE POWER OF EMPATHY

"Empathy is seeing with the eyes of another, listening with the ears of another, and feeling with the heart of another."
— Alfred Adler

Learn:

Empathy is about understanding and sharing the feelings of another person. It helps us build stronger, healthier relationships by showing others that we care about their experiences. When we use empathy, we approach situations with kindness and understanding rather than using control or intimidation.

The Yellow Truck metaphor helps us see what happens when we use toughness to get our way. Imagine a big yellow Tonka truck crushing a small red ute. The yellow truck represents using intimidation and power to control others, forcing them into submission. While it might seem like an easy way to get people to follow directions, it crushes relationships and leaves the other person feeling powerless. Instead of fostering trust and connection, it creates fear and distance.

In contrast, empathy is the opposite of the yellow truck approach. It involves listening, understanding, and connecting with the other person, ensuring that you're not "crushing" them in the process. By choosing empathy over control, you build relationships that are strong and based on mutual respect.

Consider:

In class, a student is upset after receiving a low grade on a test. Instead of using the yellow truck approach—telling the student to stop whining and study harder—the teacher takes a moment to empathise. The teacher says, "I can see you're frustrated, and it's okay to feel that way. Let's figure out how we can help you improve for the next test." This shows the student that their feelings matter, and it opens up a conversation about growth rather than shutting it down with control or intimidation.

Let's Make It Real:

Invite students to talk to the person next to them about a time when they either used empathy in a situation or experienced the yellow truck approach. How did empathy change the outcome compared to control or intimidation?

Discuss:

- How does empathy strengthen relationships, while intimidation weakens them?

- Can you think of a time when someone used empathy to help you, and how did it make you feel?
- Why is it important to avoid using the yellow truck approach in your relationships with others?

Connect:

- How do you think you're going with this skill in your own life?
- If you had to give yourself a score out of 10 (10 being awesome), what would you give yourself?
- Can you think of someone who's really good at this? What do they do that stands out to you?
- What's one small thing you can try this week to bump your score up by one point?

Do:

This week, practice using empathy in your relationships. When someone is upset or going through a hard time, take a moment to listen and understand their feelings instead of reacting with control or frustration. Reflect on how this helps you build stronger, more respectful relationships.

End-of-Week Reflection:

At the end of the week, ask yourself:

- When did I choose empathy instead of reacting with frustration or control this week, and what difference did it make?

- How did showing empathy help strengthen one of my relationships?

- What's one way I can practise empathy more next week, especially when I feel tempted to use the "yellow truck" approach?

WEEK 4:

TALKING WITH KINDNESS
AND SHOWING LOVE

*"The way we communicate with others and with ourselves
ultimately determines the quality of our lives."*
—Tony Robbins

Learn:

Effective communication is key to building strong relationships, but
it's not just about words. Everyone has different ways of expressing
and receiving love, care, and support, which are known as the **five
love languages**. These love languages help us understand how others
feel appreciated and connected. When we communicate in a way that
aligns with someone's love language, we create deeper, more meaningful
connections.

The **five love languages** are:

1. **Quality Time**: Spending focused, uninterrupted time with someone to show they matter.

2. **Gifts**: Giving thoughtful items that show care and consideration.

3. **Acts of Service**: Doing something helpful for another person to show support.

4. **Touch**: Appropriate physical touch, like a hug or pat on the back, to express affection.

5. **Words of Affirmation**: Using kind, encouraging words to uplift and validate others.

Understanding these love languages helps us communicate more effectively, as we learn to express our care in ways that others value most. It also helps us appreciate how others are showing us care, even if their love language is different from our own.

Consider:

In a group project, one student feels appreciated when their classmate spends extra time reviewing the work with them(quality time), while another student feels supported when someone helps them organize materials (acts of service). By understanding each other's love languages, the students learn to express their care in ways that resonate with their classmates, strengthening both their communication and their connection.

Let's Make It Real:

Invite students to talk to the person next to them about which love language resonates with them the most. How do they like to receive care and support? Discuss how understanding each other's love languages could improve communication and relationships.

Discuss:

- Why is it important to understand the different ways people give and receive love and care?
- Can you think of a time when someone communicated their care for you in a way that matched your love language? How did it make you feel?
- How can you practice using the five love languages to communicate more effectively with friends, family, or classmates?

Connect:

- How do you think you're going with this skill in your own life?
- If you had to give yourself a score out of 10 (10 being awesome), what would you give yourself?
- Can you think of someone who's really good at this? What do they do that stands out to you?
- What's one small thing you can try this week to bump your score up by one point?

Do:

This week, practice identifying the love languages of the people around you. Whether it's spending quality time, offering words of affirmation, or doing an act of service, use these love languages to strengthen your communication and relationships. Reflect on how understanding someone's love language can improve your connection.

End-of-Week Reflection:

At the end of the week, ask yourself:

- Which love language did I use most this week to show kindness and care to someone?

- How did understanding or noticing someone else's love language improve our connection?

- What's one way I can use a different love language next week to strengthen a relationship?

WEEK 5:

SOLVING PROBLEMS TOGETHER

*"Peace is not the absence of conflict, but the ability to
handle conflict by peaceful means."*
—Ronald Reagan

Learn:

Conflict is a normal part of life, but how we handle it makes all the
difference. Conflict resolution is about finding solutions that work for
everyone involved, without hurting or upsetting others. It involves
listening, understanding the other person's perspective, and working
together to solve the problem. When we learn to resolve conflicts in a
respectful and peaceful way, we build stronger, healthier relationships.

Consider:

Two students in class argue over who gets to use a piece of equipment.
Instead of continuing the argument, they decide to take turns using it,

and both end up happy with the outcome. By talking through the issue calmly and finding a compromise, they resolve the conflict without damaging their friendship.

Let's Make It Real:

Invite students to talk to the person next to them about a time when they resolved a conflict peacefully. How did they reach a solution, and what did they learn from the experience?

Discuss:

- Why is it important to resolve conflicts peacefully instead of getting angry or upset?
- Can you think of a time when a conflict got worse because it wasn't handled well? How could it have been resolved better?
- What steps can you take to resolve conflicts in a peaceful way?

Connect:

- How do you think you're going with this skill in your own life?
- If you had to give yourself a score out of 10 (10 being awesome), what would you give yourself?
- Can you think of someone who's really good at this? What do they do that stands out to you?
- What's one small thing you can try this week to bump your score up by one point?

Do:

This week, if you experience conflict with a classmate, friend, or family member, focus on resolving it peacefully. Listen to their side, share your perspective calmly, and work together to find a solution. Reflect on how this helps strengthen your relationships.

End-of-Week Reflection:

- Did you use any conflict resolution skills this week? How did they help?
- Were there any conflicts that were resolved positively because of your actions?
- What did you learn about resolving conflicts peacefully?

WEEK 6:

SHOWING RESPECT FOR EVERYONE

*"When people respect you as a person, they admire you.
When they respect you as a friend, they love you. When they
respect you as a leader, they follow you."*
—John C. Maxwell

Learn:

Respecting others is about treating people with kindness, understanding, and consideration, regardless of how they treat us. We can't control how others behave, but we are responsible for how we show respect. Respect is not about demanding it from others but about showing it in our actions, words, and attitudes. When we choose to respect others, we help create a positive environment and build stronger relationships, even if the same respect is not always returned.

Consider:

In class, one student disagrees with another's point of view, but instead of being dismissive or rude, they listen carefully and respond politely. Even though they don't agree, the respectful interaction leads to a thoughtful conversation. By focusing on their own behaviour, the student shows respect regardless of whether it's returned.

Let's Make It Real:

Invite students to talk to the person next to them about a time when they showed respect to someone, even if that person wasn't being respectful to them. How did it feel, and what did they learn from the experience?

Discuss:

- Why is it important to focus on how you show respect to others rather than expecting it from them?
- Can you think of a time when showing respect made a situation better, even if others didn't act respectfully?
- How can managing your own respect toward others improve your relationships?

Connect:

- How do you think you're going with this skill in your own life?
- If you had to give yourself a score out of 10 (10 being awesome), what would you give yourself?
- Can you think of someone who's really good at this? What do they do that stands out to you?

- What's one small thing you can try this week to bump your score up by one point?

Do:

This week, focus on how you show respect to others, regardless of how they act. Notice how treating others with respect changes your interactions and helps create a more positive environment.

End-of-Week Reflection:

- How did you manage your own respect toward others this week?
- Were there times when showing respect changed how someone responded to you?
- What did you learn about the importance of respecting others, regardless of their actions?

WEEK 7:

BETTER TOGETHER

"Alone we can do so little; together we can do so much."
—HELEN KELLER

Learn:

Teamwork and collaboration are about working together with others to achieve a common goal. When we collaborate, we bring our individual strengths and ideas to the table, making the group stronger. Successful teamwork involves listening to others, sharing responsibilities, and supporting each other. By working as a team, we can achieve more than we could on our own, and we build strong, trusting relationships along the way.

Consider:

During a class project, a group of students works together to complete their task. Each student has a different role, but they communicate and collaborate to make sure everyone's contributions are valued. By working as a team, they finish the project on time and feel proud of what they achieved together.

Let's Make It Real:

Invite students to talk to the person next to them about a time when they worked as part of a team. What role did they play, and how did working together help them achieve their goal?

Discuss:

- Why is teamwork important in school, sports, and other group activities?
- Can you think of a time when teamwork helped you succeed? What made the collaboration work well?
- How can you be a better team player in the classroom or on the playground?

Connect:

- How do you think you're going with this skill in your own life?
- If you had to give yourself a score out of 10 (10 being awesome), what would you give yourself?
- Can you think of someone who's really good at this? What do they do that stands out to you?
- What's one small thing you can try this week to bump your score up by one point?

Do:

This week, focus on being a supportive and active team player in your group activities. Listen to others, share responsibilities, and encourage your teammates. Notice how teamwork helps you achieve more together.

End-of-Week Reflection:

- How did teamwork help you achieve your goals this week?
- What role did you play in your team, and how did collaboration make a difference?
- What did you learn about the value of working together?

WEEK 8:

BUILDING TRUST

"Trust doesn't mean that you trust that someone won't screw up—it means you trust them when they do screw up."
—ED CATMULL

Learn:

Trust is the foundation of any strong relationship, but it's not something that's built overnight. Building and protecting trust is part of a lifelong journey of connection. Just like any relationship, trust needs continuous care, effort, and protection. Once trust is established, it must be nurtured over time to stay strong. It's not just about earning trust once—it's about showing up consistently, acting with integrity, and proving yourself reliable again and again.

Building connection is not a one-time event; it's a lifelong process. As you grow and your relationships evolve, you'll continue to learn how to strengthen and protect the connections you build. There will be times when trust is tested, and how you respond during those times is key to maintaining a strong connection.

Consider:

Imagine a student who has worked hard to build trust with their teacher by consistently turning in homework and participating in class. But one day, they forget to complete an assignment. Instead of hiding it or making excuses, the student takes responsibility, apologizes, and makes a plan to turn it in the next day. This act of owning up to the mistake helps protect the trust they've built, showing that the connection is important to them. Trust was tested, but by taking the right steps, the student reinforces the strength of the relationship.

Let's Make It Real:

Invite students to talk to the person next to them about a time when they had to rebuild or protect trust in a relationship. How did they handle the situation, and what did they learn about the ongoing journey of building trust?

Discuss:

- Why is trust something that needs to be built and protected over time?

- Can you think of a time when you earned someone's trust? How did you maintain that trust after it was built?

- What are some ways you can protect and nurture the trust in your relationships, knowing that connection is a lifelong journey?

Connect:

- How do you think you're going with this skill in your own life?
- If you had to give yourself a score out of 10 (10 being awesome), what would you give yourself?
- Can you think of someone who's really good at this? What do they do that stands out to you?
- What's one small thing you can try this week to bump your score up by one point?

Do:

This week, focus on consistently building and protecting trust in your relationships. Pay attention to how you show up for others and take steps to protect the connections you've made. Reflect on how these small, consistent actions strengthen your relationships over time.

End-of-Week Reflection:

At the end of the week, ask yourself:

- When was trust tested in one of my relationships this week, and how did I respond?
- What choices did I make that helped build or protect trust with someone else?
- What's one thing I can do next week to keep showing up as trustworthy and consistent?

WEEK 9:

RESPONSIBLE AND CONNECTED

"You can't have a strong relationship without taking responsibility for your words and actions."
—Gary Chapman

Learn:

In relationships, there is often a tension or polarity between responsibility (what we are accountable for) and the quality of the relationship (how connected we feel to the other person). Learning to balance these two forces is crucial to building and maintaining strong, healthy relationships.

On one side of the polarity, responsibility means being accountable for our actions, decisions, and behaviour. It's about showing up consistently and taking ownership when things go wrong. On the other side, relationship is about nurturing connection, trust, and communication.

It involves being compassionate, listening, and fostering mutual understanding.

The key to balancing these two forces is understanding that both are essential. Focusing too much on responsibility can make a relationship feel like a duty, causing it to become rigid or distant. However, focusing only on the relationship without accountability can lead to a lack of trust or progress. A healthy balance ensures that both accountability and connection are valued and maintained.

Consider:

Imagine two classmates working on a group project. One is very focused on getting the work done and takes full responsibility for the task, but in the process, they neglect the relationship with their partner by not listening to their ideas or collaborating. The other classmate focuses only on keeping the relationship positive and avoids giving any feedback, even when the work isn't meeting expectations. In this scenario, both responsibility and relationship suffer because they haven't found a balance.

Now, picture the same students balancing the two forces. One classmate ensures they complete their part of the work but also checks in with their partner, asking for their ideas and contributions. The other classmate takes responsibility for their share of the project while ensuring the partnership remains positive and collaborative. In this situation, the balance of responsibility and relationship strengthens both the work and the connection between them.

Let's Make It Real:

Invite students to talk to the person next to them about a time when they felt the balance between responsibility and relationship was off in a friendship or working relationship. How did that imbalance affect the situation? Discuss how balancing the two could have improved the outcome.

Discuss:

- Why is it important to balance both responsibility and relationship in our interactions with others?
- Can you think of a time when you felt responsible but neglected the relationship? How did that impact the connection?
- What are some practical ways you can make sure you are balancing responsibility with relationship in your daily life?

Connect:

- How do you think you're going with this skill in your own life?
- If you had to give yourself a score out of 10 (10 being awesome), what would you give yourself?
- Can you think of someone who's really good at this? What do they do that stands out to you?
- What's one small thing you can try this week to bump your score up by one point?

Do:

This week, focus on balancing responsibility and relationship in your interactions. Whether working on a project, helping a friend, or dealing with a conflict, ask yourself if you're maintaining both accountability for your actions and nurturing the relationship. Reflect on how this balance improves your connections with others.

End-of-Week Reflection:

At the end of the week, ask yourself:

- How did I take ownership of my actions this week?
- What situations allowed me to practice balancing responsibility and relationship, and how did it impact others?
- What have I learned about balancing responsibility and connection that I can apply moving forward?

WEEK 10:

SUPPORTIVE FRIENDSHIPS USING THE EMPOWERMENT MODEL

"A friend is someone who gives you total freedom to be yourself."
—JIM MORRISON

Learn:

Being a supportive friend is about more than just helping someone; it's about empowering them to solve problems and grow. The Empowerment Model can help you support your friends in a way that gives them the tools to handle challenges on their own. Instead of fixing their problems for them, you can guide them through these six steps:

1. **Empathy**: Start by acknowledging their feelings with something like, "Oh no, I can see how that's tough." This shows that you care and understand their situation.

2. **Empower**: Ask your friend, "What are you going to do?" This question helps them realise they have the power to make decisions.

3. **Explore**: Encourage them to reflect on their past efforts by asking, "What have you tried so far?"

4. **Educate**: Offer guidance without taking over, saying, "I have some ideas if you'd like to hear them," so they feel supported but still in control.

5. **Expect**: Help them take ownership by asking, "What will you do now?"

6. **Encourage**: Finally, support them by saying, "Let me know how it goes." This shows you're there for them and invested in their progress.

Using this model in your friendships helps your friends feel supported while empowering them to take action and grow through their challenges.

Consider:

Imagine your friend is upset because they had a conflict with a classmate. Instead of telling them what to do, you walk them through the Empowerment Model.

- First, you show Empathy by saying, "Oh no, I'm sorry that happened. That sounds really frustrating."

- Then, you Empower them: "What are you thinking of doing next?"

- You Explore with them: "What have you tried already to make it better?"

- You Educate gently: "I have some ideas that might help, but only if you want to hear them."
- Once they've thought it through, you set an Expectation: "So what are you going to do now?"
- Finally, you Encourage: "Let me know how it goes, and I'm here if you need anything."

By using the Empowerment Model, you help your friend feel capable and supported, instead of solving the problem for them.

Let's Make It Real:

Invite students to talk to the person next to them about a time when they supported a friend. How could they have used the Empowerment Model to help their friend take control of the situation?

Discuss:

- How does using the Empowerment Model in friendships make you a more supportive friend?
- Can you think of a time when asking someone, "What are you going to do?" helped them feel more empowered?
- What are some situations where you can use this model to help your friends take ownership of their challenges?

Connect:

- How do you think you're going with this skill in your own life?
- If you had to give yourself a score out of 10 (10 being awesome), what would you give yourself?

- Can you think of someone who's really good at this? What do they do that stands out to you?
- What's one small thing you can try this week to bump your score up by one point?

Do:

This week, practice supporting a friend using the Empowerment Model. When they face a challenge, guide them through the steps: Empathy, Empower, Explore, Educate, Expect, and Encourage. Notice how this approach helps them feel more confident and in control.

End of Week Reflection:

At the end of the week, ask yourself:

- When did I use the Empowerment Model to support a friend this week, and how did it help them?
- How did asking questions instead of giving answers change the way my friend handled their problem?
- What's one way I can keep building supportive friendships by using the Empowerment Model next week?

PART TWO

BUILDING JOYFUL RESPONSIBILITY

In this section, students will discover that taking responsibility for their actions doesn't have to feel like a heavy burden—in fact, it can be something that brings confidence, growth, and even joy!

Through simple, real-life lessons and meaningful conversations, students will learn that responsibility isn't just about following rules—it's about making thoughtful choices, owning their part, and understanding how their actions affect others.

We want students to see responsibility as something *they* get to carry with pride—not something that's forced on them. When we choose to be responsible, we build trust, grow stronger relationships, and learn more about who we are and who we want to become.

WEEK 11:

OWNING YOUR ACTIONS

"Responsibility equals accountability equals ownership.
And a sense of ownership is the most powerful
weapon a team or organization can have."
—Pat Summitt

Learn:

Taking ownership of our actions is a key way to step into being powerful. When we take responsibility, we acknowledge that we have the ability to change and influence situations. A powerful person recognises their role in both success and failure and uses this understanding to grow. In contrast, a powerless mindset blames others or circumstances and avoids responsibility, limiting personal growth. Owning your actions shows that you're taking control of your choices and helps build trust with others.

Consider:

During a group project, Lucy forgot to bring her materials for the presentation, which impacted the entire group's grade. Instead of blaming her groupmates for not reminding her or making excuses about her busy schedule, Lucy admits her mistake and takes ownership. By acting powerfully, she acknowledges her role and offers to do extra work to make up for it, restoring trust with her groupmates. A powerless response would have been to shift the blame or deny responsibility, which would have further damaged the group's trust.

Let's Make It Real:

Invite students to talk to the person next to them about a time when they felt powerful by taking responsibility for their actions or when they felt powerless by avoiding responsibility. How did this affect the situation?

Discuss:

- Can you think of a time when you didn't take ownership of your actions? How did it affect others?
- Why do you think it's sometimes difficult to take responsibility when things go wrong?
- How does it feel when someone else admits they were wrong? Does it make you respect them more or less? Why?

Connect:

- How do you think you're going with this skill in your own life?
- If you had to give yourself a score out of 10 (10 being awesome), what would you give yourself?

- Can you think of someone who's really good at this? What do they do that stands out to you?
- What's one small thing you can try this week to bump your score up by one point?

Do:

This week, focus on being powerful by taking ownership of your actions. If something goes wrong, instead of blaming others or making excuses, own your part in it. Share how it felt to take responsibility and what you learned from the experience.

End-of-Week Reflection:

At the end of the week, ask yourself:

- How did I take ownership of my actions this week?
- What situations allowed me to practice responsibility, and how did it impact others?
- What have I learned about owning my actions that I can apply moving forward?

WEEK 12:

POWERFUL PEOPLE, POWERFUL RELATIONSHIPS

"Powerful people do not try to control other people.
They know it doesn't work, and that it's not their job.
Their job is to control themselves."
—DANNY SILK

Learn:

In every relationship, there are different ways we can relate to each other based on how we feel about ourselves. The way we relate to others can be described as either powerful or powerless, and these dynamics shape how we interact.

There are three main types of relating:

1. **Powerless + Powerless = Controlling**
   When both people in a relationship feel powerless, they often try to control each other. This creates a relationship full of conflict,

where both people try to feel more in control by pushing the other person down. It leads to arguments and manipulation, but it doesn't create real connection.

2. **Powerless + Powerful = Codependent**
   In this dynamic, one person feels powerless and the other feels powerful. The powerless person depends on the powerful one to make decisions, manage situations, and control outcomes. This creates a codependent relationship, where one person relies too much on the other, and there's no balance.

3. **Powerful + Powerful = Freedom**
   In this healthy dynamic, both people feel powerful. They know they can make their own decisions, and they don't need to control or depend on others. This creates a relationship of freedom, where each person respects the other and works together, knowing they're responsible for their own actions.

Being powerful means taking responsibility for yourself and your choices, while being powerless leads to blaming others, avoiding responsibility, or feeling like you don't have control.

Consider:

Two students are paired for a class project. In one pair, both students feel powerless and try to control each other. This leads to frustration and arguments as they both feel like the other person isn't doing their part. In another pair, one student feels powerful and takes over the project, while the other student feels powerless and just follows along, leading to a codependent dynamic.

But in a powerful + powerful dynamic, both students work together, knowing that each is responsible for their part. They collaborate freely, respecting each other's ideas and decisions. This creates a healthy, balanced relationship where both students feel empowered.

Let's Make It Real:

Invite students to talk to the person next to them about a time when they felt either powerful or powerless in a relationship. How did that dynamic affect the way they related to the other person?

Discuss:

- What does it mean to be powerful in a relationship, and how is it different from being powerless?
- Can you think of a time when a relationship felt controlling or codependent? How did that affect you?
- How can you work toward more powerful + powerful relationships where both people have freedom and respect?

Connect:

- How do you think you're going with this skill in your own life?
- If you had to give yourself a score out of 10 (10 being awesome), what would you give yourself?
- Can you think of someone who's really good at this? What do they do that stands out to you?
- What's one small thing you can try this week to bump your score up by one point?

Do:

This week, focus on building powerful relationships. In your interactions with friends, classmates, or family members, pay attention to whether you're acting from a place of power or feeling powerless. Practice taking responsibility for your actions and respecting others' decisions to create more freedom and balance.

End-of-Week Reflection:

At the end of the week, ask yourself:

- When did I act as a powerful person in a relationship this week, and how did it change the way things went?
- Did I notice any times when I felt powerless or tried to control others? What happened?
- What's one thing I can do next week to build more "powerful + powerful" relationships?

WEEK 13:

CHOOSE LOVE OVER FEAR

"There are only two emotions: love and fear. All positive emotions come from love, all negative emotions from fear. From love flows happiness, contentment, peace, and joy. From fear comes anger, hate, anxiety, and guilt. It's true that there are only two primary emotions, love and fear. But it's more accurate to say that there is only love or fear, for we cannot feel these two emotions together, at exactly the same time."
—ELISABETH KÜBLER-ROSS

Learn:

In our relationships and interactions, we often respond either out of fear or out of love. These two forces shape how we connect with others—or how we become disconnected. Fear causes us to protect ourselves, creating distance and disconnection. When we act out of fear, we avoid vulnerability, hide our mistakes, and sometimes push people away to feel safe. Fear drives us to control situations because we're afraid of being hurt, judged, or misunderstood.

On the other hand, love creates connection. Acting from love means choosing to trust, be vulnerable, and seek understanding. When we choose love, we open up to others, allowing deeper, more meaningful relationships to form. Love fosters a sense of safety, where people feel seen, heard, and valued. It encourages growth because it's based on support rather than control.

The key difference between fear and love is how they affect relationships:

- Fear drives self-protection and distance. It keeps us focused on defending ourselves, often at the cost of connection with others.
- Love drives connection. It allows us to be open, understanding, and supportive, even when mistakes are made.

When we choose love over fear, we create a space where trust can grow, and relationships can thrive.

Fear vs Love:

- **Fear**: "If I don't protect myself, I might get hurt."
- **Love**: "I choose to trust and connect, knowing that mistakes and misunderstandings are part of growth."

Consider:

A student is afraid to share their opinion during a group discussion because they worry about being judged. Acting from fear, the student stays silent and disconnects from the group. The teacher, noticing this, decides to address the situation with love rather than control or frustration. The teacher says, "I'd love to hear what you think, and this is a safe space for you to share without judgment." By using love to create a safe environment, the teacher encourages the student to open up and connect with the group.

Let's Make It Real:

Invite students to talk to the person next to them about a time when they responded to a situation out of fear and how it led to distance or disconnection. Then, discuss a time when they acted out of love and how that helped build connection. How did these different responses shape their relationships?

Discuss:

- How does fear lead to self-protection and disconnection, while love builds trust and connection?
- Can you think of a time when someone used love to guide your behaviour, and how did that impact your relationship with them?
- What are some ways you can choose love when interacting with others, especially when it feels easier to react out of fear?

Connect:

- How do you think you're going with this skill in your own life?
- If you had to give yourself a score out of 10 (10 being awesome), what would you give yourself?
- Can you think of someone who's really good at this? What do they do that stands out to you?
- What's one small thing you can try this week to bump your score up by one point?

Do:

This week, practice choosing love over fear in your interactions. When faced with a challenge or conflict, ask yourself whether you're responding out of self-protection or connection. Choose to respond with love, seeking to understand and build trust rather than create distance. Reflect on how this approach affects your relationships.

End-of-Week Reflection:

At the end of the week, ask yourself:

- When did I notice myself reacting out of fear this week, and what happened in that situation?

- When did I choose love instead of fear, and how did it help me feel more connected?

- What's one way I can remind myself to choose love over fear next week?

WEEK 14:

FREEDOM THROUGH BOUNDARIES

"Boundaries define us. They define what is me and what is not me.
A boundary shows me where I end and someone else begins,
leading me to a sense of ownership."
—Dr. John Townsend and Dr. Henry Cloud

Learn:

Boundaries help us know where our responsibilities lie and what we should protect in our lives. Freedom doesn't mean we can do whatever we want; instead, it means we have the ability to make choices within clear boundaries. These boundaries create safety, trust, and respect in our relationships, allowing us to thrive. When we understand and respect boundaries, we feel free to make good choices without fear or confusion.

Consider:

In a classroom, students may feel like following rules limits their freedom, but in reality, these rules (boundaries) allow everyone to learn in a safe environment. For example, during free play, students are told not to run in certain areas. This isn't meant to restrict their fun, but to ensure everyone's safety. When students respect the boundaries, everyone enjoys the time together without injuries or disruptions.

Let's Make It Real:

Invite students to talk to the person next to them and discuss a time when respecting a boundary gave them more freedom to make better choices. How did it impact their experience?

Discuss:

- Can you think of a time when you didn't like a boundary but later realised it helped you?
- How do boundaries create safety in a classroom or on the playground?
- What happens when we don't respect boundaries?

Connect:

- How do you think you're going with this skill in your own life?
- If you had to give yourself a score out of 10 (10 being awesome), what would you give yourself?
- Can you think of someone who's really good at this? What do they do that stands out to you?

- What's one small thing you can try this week to bump your score up by one point?

Do:

This week, notice a boundary in your classroom, home, or playground and think about how it helps create freedom. Try to follow that boundary with a positive attitude, and reflect on how it improves your experience.

End-of-Week Reflection:

- How did respecting boundaries give you more freedom this week?
- Can you share a time when a boundary helped you make a better choice?
- What did you learn about how boundaries help create freedom?

WEEK 15:

RESPECT AND CONNECT

"Respect is one of the greatest expressions of love and leadership."
—John C. Maxwell

Learn:

Respecting others is about treating people with kindness, understanding, and consideration, regardless of how they treat you. When we show respect, we create strong, durable relationships, but when respect is lacking, relationships become fragile and easily broken. The tissue and rope metaphor helps us understand this idea.

Tissue-thin relationships are fragile and can't handle much stress because respect isn't always present on both sides. These relationships tear apart easily when things get difficult. In contrast, rope relationships are strong and durable. In these relationships, both people hold their end of the rope, showing mutual respect and support. You are only responsible for your end of the rope, but the strength of the relationship depends on both people holding on.

Respecting others, even when they don't respect you, strengthens your end of the rope and keeps your side of the relationship strong, regardless of how the other person behaves.

Consider:

In class, one student feels frustrated with a classmate who interrupts during group discussions. Instead of reacting rudely or disrespectfully, the student holds their end of the rope by calmly explaining how the interruptions make it difficult to focus. By managing their own respect toward the classmate, the student keeps the relationship strong on their side, even though the other person hasn't yet changed their behaviour. This keeps the relationship from becoming tissue-thin and helps maintain a positive connection.

Let's Make It Real:

Invite students to talk to the person next to them about a time when they felt they were holding their end of the rope in a relationship, even when the other person wasn't. How did managing their own respect affect the relationship?

Discuss:

- Why is it important to hold your end of the rope, even when the other person doesn't?
- Can you think of a time when a relationship felt tissue-thin because of a lack of respect? How did it affect you?

- What can you do to turn a tissue-thin relationship into a rope relationship by showing respect?

Connect:

- How do you think you're going with this skill in your own life?
- If you had to give yourself a score out of 10 (10 being awesome), what would you give yourself?
- Can you think of someone who's really good at this? What do they do that stands out to you?
- What's one small thing you can try this week to bump your score up by one point?

Do:

This week, focus on strengthening your end of the rope in your relationships. Whether it's a classmate, friend, or family member, take responsibility for showing respect, even if the other person isn't holding their end. Reflect on how this helps keep your relationships strong.

End of Week Reflection:

At the end of the week, ask yourself:

- Did I show respect in a relationship this week, even when it was difficult? How did it affect the connection?
- Which of my relationships felt more like "rope" and which felt more like "tissue"? What made the difference?
- What's one thing I can do next week to strengthen my end of the rope in an important relationship?

WEEK 16:

GROWING AND TAKING RESPONSIBILITY

"You cannot change your destination overnight,
but you can change your direction overnight."
—Jim Rohn

Learn:

Taking responsibility for your own growth means recognising that you have the power to shape your future through the choices you make. The Empowerment Model can help guide you in this process by breaking down personal responsibility into six manageable steps:

1. **Empathy**: Start by acknowledging your current situation. Say to yourself, "Oh no, I'm not where I want to be yet," which helps you face reality with honesty.

2. **Empower**: Ask, "What am I going to do to improve?" This reminds you that you have control over your next steps.

3. **Explore**: Reflect on what you've tried so far by asking, "What have I done to grow or change?" This helps you assess your progress and identify areas to improve.

4. **Educate**: Seek advice or resources by saying, "If you have any ideas, I want to hear them," allowing you to gather insights while still taking control of your growth.

5. **Expect**: After gathering information and reflecting, ask, "What will I do now?" This is where you take ownership of your next steps.

6. **Encourage**: Finally, remind yourself, "Let me check in on my progress." This helps you stay accountable and ensures that you keep moving forward.

Using the Empowerment Model allows you to take control of your personal growth journey. By walking through these steps, you can evaluate where you are, make intentional choices, and take responsibility for improving yourself.

Consider:

Imagine you want to get better at handing your assignments in on time, but you feel like the teacher's expectations are unfair. Instead of blaming the situation, you decide to use the Empowerment Model to take responsibility for your own growth:

- **Empathy:** "Oh no, I can see I've been struggling to stay organised."

- **Empower:** "What am I going to do about it?"

- **Explore:** "What have I already tried to help myself get my work in on time?"

- **Educate:** "I might need some new strategies—what can I learn or who can I ask for ideas?"

- **Expect:** "What will I do now?" Decide on one clear action to take.

- **Encourage:** "Let me check in with myself next week to see if this new plan is working."

By walking through these steps, you take ownership of the problem, make a plan, and keep yourself accountable. This shows how the Empowerment Model can help you grow by facing your own challenges with responsibility.

Let's Make It Real:

Invite students to talk to the person next to them about a time when they needed to take responsibility for their personal growth. How could using the Empowerment Model have helped them stay on track and make better decisions?

Discuss:

- How does using the Empowerment Model help you take responsibility for your own growth?

- Can you think of a time when you needed to focus on improving yourself? What did you learn from the process?

- How can you use this model to support your friends to solve their problems?

Connect:

- How do you think you're going with this skill in your own life?
- If you had to give yourself a score out of 10 (10 being awesome), what would you give yourself?
- Can you think of someone who's really good at this? What do they do that stands out to you?
- What's one small thing you can try this week to bump your score up by one point?

Do:

This week, focus on using the Empowerment Model for your own growth. Identify an area where you want to improve, and walk through the steps: Empathy, Empower, Explore, Educate, Expect, and Encourage. Notice how this process helps you take ownership of your growth and stay accountable.

End of Week Reflection:

At the end of the week, ask yourself:

- What's one area I focused on growing in this week, and how did I take responsibility for it?
- Which step of the Empowerment Model helped me the most in staying on track with my growth?
- How did taking responsibility for my growth make a difference in how I felt or what I achieved?

WEEK 17:

LEARNING FROM MISTAKES WITH LOVE

*"Freedom is not worth having if it does not include
the freedom to make mistakes."*
—Mahatma Gandhi

Learn:

Making mistakes is part of learning and growing. When we face our mistakes, we have the opportunity to choose how we respond—whether we learn from them or let them hold us back. The message "love requires freedom, freedom requires choices, and one of those choices is love" helps us understand that love and growth come from having the freedom to make decisions, even when those decisions lead to mistakes. It's in the freedom to choose that we experience love and connection, both with ourselves and others.

Freedom gives us the space to make mistakes and grow. Without freedom, our choices wouldn't be meaningful, and without choices, love becomes control rather than a genuine connection. In relationships, whether with friends, teachers, or ourselves, love can only thrive when we have the freedom to choose it, even in the face of mistakes.

Consider:

Imagine a student who makes a mistake on a test by not studying enough. They feel embarrassed and afraid of being judged. Instead of focusing on the mistake, the teacher gives the student the freedom to choose how they want to learn from it. The teacher says, "I understand it's hard when you don't do as well as you wanted, but you have the freedom to choose how you respond. You can learn from this, and one of those choices is to show yourself love by improving next time." This shows the student that they are free to make mistakes and grow from them with love and support.

Let's Make It Real:

Invite students to talk to the person next to them about a time when they made a mistake and had the freedom to choose how to respond. How did choosing love and growth help them overcome the mistake?

Discuss:

- Why is it important to have the freedom to make mistakes in order to grow?
- Can you think of a time when someone showed you love by giving you the freedom to learn from a mistake?

- How can you show love and support to others when they make mistakes?

Connect:

- How do you think you're going with this skill in your own life?
- If you had to give yourself a score out of 10 (10 being awesome), what would you give yourself?
- Can you think of someone who's really good at this? What do they do that stands out to you?
- What's one small thing you can try this week to bump your score up by one point?

Do:

This week, if you make a mistake, remember that you have the freedom to choose how to respond. One of those choices can be love—love for yourself, others, and the process of learning. Reflect on how choosing love and growth helps you move forward after a mistake.

End-of-Week Reflection:

At the end of the week, ask yourself:

- When I made a mistake this week, how did I choose to respond—with love, growth, or frustration?
- What did I learn about myself from having the freedom to make mistakes?
- How can I show love and support to myself or others when mistakes happen in the future?

WEEK 18:

HELPING EACH OTHER GROW

"Surround yourself with only people who are going to lift you higher."
—Oprah Winfrey

Learn:

Accountability partners are people who help us stay focused on our goals and encourage us to do our best. Having someone who checks in with us, supports us, and holds us accountable can be a powerful way to stay motivated. Whether it's for schoolwork, personal goals, or good habits, working with an accountability partner helps us take responsibility for our actions and stay on track.

Consider:

In class, two students decide to become accountability partners for their reading goals. Each week, they check in with each other to make sure they've been reading for the agreed amount of time. When one student falls behind, the other encourages them to catch up. This partnership helps them both stay focused and make progress on their reading goals.

Let's Make It Real:

Invite students to talk to the person next to them about a time when having a partner helped them succeed, or when they helped someone else stay accountable. How did this partnership help them reach their goals?

Discuss:

- How can having an accountability partner help you stay focused on your goals?
- Can you think of a time when someone helped you stay on track with a goal or task?
- What qualities make a good accountability partner?

Connect:

- How do you think you're going with this skill in your own life?
- If you had to give yourself a score out of 10 (10 being awesome), what would you give yourself?
- Can you think of someone who's really good at this? What do they do that stands out to you?
- What's one small thing you can try this week to bump your score up by one point?

Do:

This week, choose an accountability partner for one of your goals, whether it's in school, sports, or your personal life. Check in with each other regularly to see how you're progressing and encourage each other to stay on track.

End-of-Week Reflection:

- How did working with an accountability partner help you this week?

- Were there times when your partner encouraged or motivated you to do better?

- What did you learn about the value of having someone hold you accountable?

WEEK 19:

STICKING WITH IT

"Discipline is the bridge between goals and accomplishment."
—JIM ROHN

Learn:

Practicing self-discipline is a hallmark of being powerful. Powerful individuals make intentional choices, even when it's hard, because they know they are in control of their actions. They don't let distractions or temporary emotions dictate their behaviour. In contrast, a powerless mindset gives in to distractions or blames circumstances, feeling like they have no control over their actions. Self-discipline gives you the ability to stay focused on your goals and take charge of your outcomes.

Consider:

A student sets a goal to finish their homework every evening before playing video games. By acting powerfully, they resist the temptation to play first and stick to their goal. Their decision to practice self-discipline helps them feel more in control and leads to better results in school. A powerless approach would have been to give in to distractions, blaming a lack of time for unfinished work.

Let's Make It Real:

Invite students to talk to the person next to them about a time when they showed self-discipline and acted powerfully. How did that choice make them feel more in control? Discuss times when they felt powerless because they gave in to distractions or external influences.

Discuss:

- Why is self-discipline important for reaching your goals?
- Can you think of a time when you struggled to stay focused on something important? What did you learn from that experience?
- How can building self-discipline help you in school, friendships, or sports?

Connect:

- How do you think you're going with this skill in your own life?
- If you had to give yourself a score out of 10 (10 being awesome), what would you give yourself?
- Can you think of someone who's really good at this? What do they do that stands out to you?
- What's one small thing you can try this week to bump your score up by one point?

Do:

This week, practice being powerful by making intentional, disciplined choices. Stay focused on your goals, resist distractions, and reflect on how this makes you feel more in control of your actions.

End-of-Week Reflection:

At the end of the week, ask yourself:

- When did I use self-discipline this week, even when I felt distracted or didn't feel like it?
- How did sticking with it help me feel more powerful or in control of my choices?
- What's one area I want to practise more self-discipline in next week, and how will it help me reach my goals?

WEEK 20:

JOYFUL RESPONSIBILITY

"With great freedom comes great responsibility."
—Eleanor Roosevelt

Learn:

Taking responsibility doesn't have to feel like a burden. In fact, when we approach responsibility with a joyful mindset, it can bring satisfaction and fulfillment. Joyful responsibility means seeing the tasks we have to do not as chores, but as opportunities to grow, contribute, and enjoy the process. Balancing work and play isn't about choosing between one or the other; it's about finding joy in taking care of your responsibilities and then enjoying your free time knowing you've done your part.

Joyful responsibility allows you to approach your schoolwork, chores, and obligations with a positive attitude. When you handle your responsibilities with joy, it gives you a sense of pride and accomplishment, and you get to enjoy your downtime even more because you know you've earned it.

Consider:

A student knows they have a big homework assignment due, but they also want to play outside with their friends. Instead of feeling like homework is a punishment, the student takes a joyful responsibility approach. They decide to work on the assignment first, knowing they'll feel proud once it's completed. By taking responsibility and finishing their work, they then get to fully enjoy playing with their friends, free from worry. The student learns that responsibility doesn't take away from fun—it enhances it.

Let's Make It Real:

Invite students to talk to the person next to them about a time when they approached responsibility with a joyful attitude. How did handling their responsibilities first help them enjoy their free time more?

Discuss:

- Why is it important to balance responsibility and fun in your daily life?
- Can you think of a time when taking responsibility helped you feel more joyful or accomplished?
- How can you find joy in completing your responsibilities, even when the tasks seem difficult?

Connect:

- How do you think you're going with this skill in your own life?
- If you had to give yourself a score out of 10 (10 being awesome), what would you give yourself?
- Can you think of someone who's really good at this? What do they do that stands out to you?
- What's one small thing you can try this week to bump your score up by one point?

Do:

This week, practice joyful responsibility by approaching your schoolwork, chores, or other obligations with a positive attitude. Notice how taking care of your responsibilities allows you to enjoy your free time more fully and with a greater sense of accomplishment.

End-of-Week Reflection:

At the end of the week, ask yourself:

- Did I approach a specific responsibility with a joyful attitude this week? How did that change the way I felt while doing it?
- How did finishing my responsibilities first affect the way I enjoyed my free time afterward?
- What's one thing I can try next week to bring more joy into the way I handle my responsibilities?

PART THREE

ACHIEVING GENUINE RESTORATION

This section is all about learning how to repair relationships when things go wrong—because let's face it, we all make mistakes sometimes.

Students will explore how to take responsibility when they've hurt someone, how to listen and make things right, and how to rebuild trust over time. Instead of focusing on blame or punishment, we'll focus on courage, honesty, and healing.

Restoration isn't about being perfect—it's about being real. When students learn how to own their part and care about how others feel, relationships grow stronger than ever. Together, we'll build a culture where making things right is seen as an act of strength, not weakness.

WEEK 21:

THE ART OF APOLOGY

"It's important to be able to say sorry, even if you find it really hard."
—Chilli (Bluey's Mom)

Learn:

Apologising is an important part of taking responsibility for our actions when we've made a mistake or hurt someone. A sincere apology shows that we understand how our actions affected others and that we're willing to make amends. It's more than just saying "sorry"—it's about acknowledging the harm done, accepting responsibility, and committing to doing better. Learning how to apologise sincerely can help repair relationships and rebuild trust.

Consider:

In the classroom, one student accidentally bumps into another and knocks their books to the ground. Instead of walking away, the student apologises, picks up the books, and checks if their classmate is okay. The apology, paired with actions to make things right, helps repair the situation quickly, and the two students continue without any resentment.

Let's Make It Real:

Invite students to talk to the person next to them about a time when they gave or received a sincere apology. How did the apology affect the situation, and what did they learn from it?

Discuss:

- Why is it important to apologise when we've made a mistake or hurt someone?
- Can you think of a time when someone's apology helped fix a difficult situation?
- What are the key elements of a sincere apology, and how can they make it more meaningful?

Connect:

- How do you think you're going with this skill in your own life?
- If you had to give yourself a score out of 10 (10 being awesome), what would you give yourself?
- Can you think of someone who's really good at this? What do they do that stands out to you?
- What's one small thing you can try this week to bump your score up by one point?

Do:

This week, if you realise you've made a mistake or hurt someone, practise giving a sincere apology. Take responsibility for your actions, and ask how you can make it right. Notice how this helps repair the relationship and build trust.

End-of-Week Reflection:

- Did you give or receive an apology this week? How did it affect the situation?
- What did a sincere apology teach you about restoring trust and relationships?
- What did you learn about the importance of apologising when you've made a mistake?

WEEK 22:

FORGIVENESS AND
MOVING FORWARD

"Forgiveness is not an occasional act; it is a permanent attitude."
—Martin Luther King Jr.

Learn:

Forgiveness is the act of letting go of resentment or anger toward someone who has hurt or wronged us. It doesn't mean forgetting what happened or excusing bad behaviour, but it does mean releasing the negative emotions tied to the situation so we can move forward in peace. Forgiving others helps us heal and prevents bitterness from damaging our relationships. When we choose to forgive, we free ourselves from holding onto past hurt and open the door for reconciliation and growth.

Consider:

In class, two students argue and stop talking to each other. After a few days, one student decides to apologise, and the other accepts the apology. They forgive each other and move past the argument, restoring their friendship. By choosing forgiveness, they let go of the negative feelings and continue to support each other as friends.

Let's Make It Real:

Invite students to talk to the person next to them about a time when they forgave someone or were forgiven by someone else. How did the act of forgiveness help them move forward?

Discuss:

- Why is forgiveness important for healing relationships and moving forward?
- Can you think of a time when forgiving someone helped you feel better or restored a friendship?
- How can holding onto anger or resentment hurt both you and your relationships?

Connect:

- How do you think you're going with this skill in your own life?
- If you had to give yourself a score out of 10 (10 being awesome), what would you give yourself?
- Can you think of someone who's really good at this? What do they do that stands out to you?
- What's one small thing you can try this week to bump your score up by one point?

Do:

This week, if someone hurts or wrongs you, practise forgiveness. Let go of any negative feelings, and if it's appropriate, talk to the person and let them know you forgive them. Notice how this brings peace and helps you move forward.

End-of-Week Reflection:

- Did I choose to forgive someone this week? How did it change the way I felt afterward?
- What difference did forgiveness make in my friendship or connection with others?
- Is there anyone I still need to forgive so I can move forward with peace?

WEEK 23:

RESTORING TRUST

*"Trust is choosing to make something important to you
vulnerable to the actions of someone else."*
—Brené Brown

Learn:

Trust can be easily damaged when there's conflict or a mistake, but it's not impossible to rebuild. Restoring trust requires time, consistent actions, and a genuine effort to make things right. When we are patient, honest, and committed to showing we've changed, we can rebuild trust and repair damaged relationships. This process often requires both parties to communicate openly, forgive, and commit to working on the relationship.

Consider:

Two classmates have an argument, and one feels hurt because the other shared something personal that wasn't meant to be shared.

After realising the mistake, the student apologises and works hard to show that they can be trusted again. Over time, they prove that they've learned from the situation, and the trust between them slowly starts to rebuild. Both students communicate and show patience, allowing their friendship to recover.

Let's Make It Real:

Invite students to talk to the person next to them about a time when they had to work to restore trust after a conflict or mistake. How did they rebuild the trust, and what steps did they take?

Discuss:

- Why is it important to work on rebuilding trust after it's been broken?
- Can you think of a time when someone's consistent actions helped you trust them again?
- What steps can you take to restore trust if you've hurt someone or broken their trust?

Connect:

- How do you think you're going with this skill in your own life?
- If you had to give yourself a score out of 10 (10 being awesome), what would you give yourself?
- Can you think of someone who's really good at this? What do they do that stands out to you?
- What's one small thing you can try this week to bump your score up by one point?

Do:

This week, focus on restoring trust if there's been a conflict or broken trust with someone. Be consistent, honest, and patient in your actions, and notice how these efforts help rebuild the relationship over time.

End-of-Week Reflection:

- Were there any situations where you worked to restore trust this week? How did it go?

- What actions did you take to show that you were committed to rebuilding trust?

- What did you learn about the process of restoring trust after a conflict?

WEEK 24:

SECOND CHANCES

"Don't think there are no second chances. Life always offers you a second chance . . . It's called tomorrow."
—Nicholas Sparks

Learn:

Second chances are about giving someone the opportunity to correct their mistakes and grow from them. We all make mistakes, and sometimes we need another chance to show that we've learned and can do better. Offering second chances helps build trust and allows people to improve, but it also means setting healthy boundaries to avoid repeating the same mistakes. Giving someone a second chance can lead to personal growth and stronger relationships.

Consider:

A student is given another chance to redo a homework assignment after not doing their best the first time. With the second chance, they put in more effort and end up producing a much better result. The opportunity to try again helps them learn and take more responsibility for their work.

Let's Make It Real:

Invite students to talk to the person next to them about a time when they were given a second chance or when they gave someone else a second chance. How did it change the situation, and what did they learn?

Discuss:

- Why are second chances important for personal growth and learning from mistakes?
- Can you think of a time when a second chance helped you or someone else improve?
- How can we offer second chances in a way that encourages responsibility and growth?

Connect:

- How do you think you're going with this skill in your own life?
- If you had to give yourself a score out of 10 (10 being awesome), what would you give yourself?
- Can you think of someone who's really good at this? What do they do that stands out to you?
- What's one small thing you can try this week to bump your score up by one point?

Do:

This week, if someone makes a mistake, consider offering them a second chance. Help them understand what went wrong and encourage them to do better next time. Notice how second chances allow people to grow and improve their actions.

End-of-Week Reflection:

- Did you offer someone a second chance this week, or were you given one?
- How did a second chance change the outcome of a situation?
- What did you learn about the value of second chances in relationships?

WEEK 25:

TAKING RESPONSIBILITY
IN FRIENDSHIPS

"If you own this story, you get to write the ending."
—Brené Brown

Learn:

All relationships face challenges, and there will be times when connections are strained or damaged. Repairing relationships is a crucial part of the lifelong journey of building and protecting connections. When something goes wrong, it's not the end of the relationship—it's an opportunity to learn, grow, and strengthen the connection by repairing the trust and communication that may have been broken.

Repairing relationships is about acknowledging mistakes, offering and accepting apologies, and committing to rebuilding the connection. Understanding that relationships are constantly evolving helps us see that every repair is part of the larger journey of connection. Each time we take steps to heal a relationship, we show that we value it and are willing to put in the effort to protect it.

Consider:

Two friends have an argument because one of them didn't show up to an important event. The hurt caused by this breaks their connection for a while. But instead of letting the relationship remain damaged, they decide to talk it through. The friend who missed the event apologises and explains why they couldn't make it. The other friend listens and forgives. Through open communication and a willingness to repair, they rebuild their relationship. This moment becomes a step forward in their lifelong journey of staying connected.

Let's Make It Real:

Invite students to talk to the person next to them about a time when they had to repair a relationship. What steps did they take to rebuild the connection, and how did this experience help them understand that relationships are an ongoing journey?

Discuss:

- Why is repairing relationships an important part of the journey of connection?

- Can you think of a time when you had to repair a relationship? How did that affect your understanding of what it means to protect and rebuild trust?

- How can you approach future relationship challenges, knowing that building and protecting connection is a lifelong journey?

Connect:

- How do you think you're going with this skill in your own life?
- If you had to give yourself a score out of 10 (10 being awesome), what would you give yourself?
- Can you think of someone who's really good at this? What do they do that stands out to you?
- What's one small thing you can try this week to bump your score up by one point?

Do:

This week, focus on relationships that may need repair. Reach out to those with whom your connection has been strained, and take steps to rebuild trust and communication. Remember that repairing relationships is part of the lifelong journey of maintaining and protecting your connections.

End-of-Week Reflection:

At the end of the week, ask yourself:

- Did I have a moment this week where I needed to repair a friendship? What step did I take to make it right?
- How did taking responsibility for my actions affect my friendship and the way my friend felt?
- What's one thing I can keep doing to protect and strengthen my friendships, even when things go wrong?

WEEK 26:

POWERFUL FRIENDSHIPS

*"Your reputation is what people say about you when
you're not in the room."*
—JEFF BEZOS

Learn:

Our reputation is built on how we consistently show up in the world—
our actions, words, and behaviour shape how others perceive us. One
of the key factors that can damage our reputation is falling into the
irresponsibility cycle, where we take on roles that avoid personal responsibility and shift blame to others.

The irresponsibility cycle includes three roles:

1. **Victim**: The victim believes that everything happens to them,
   and they are powerless to change it. In relationships, the victim
   blames others for their problems, damaging trust and accountability.

2. **Caregiver/Rescuer**: The rescuer steps in to "save" others, often taking responsibility for problems that aren't theirs. This can lead to resentment and a lack of accountability in the relationship, as the rescuer removes responsibility from the person who needs to learn from their mistakes.

3. **Bad Guy**: The bad guy is blamed for everything going wrong, and this person either accepts blame unfairly or lashes out in frustration. This role damages relationships and perpetuates negative perceptions.

Breaking the irresponsibility cycle is essential for building a positive reputation. By taking responsibility for our actions, we step out of these roles and into a place of empowerment. A positive reputation is built on accountability, integrity, and showing up in relationships with responsibility, not blame.

Consider:

Imagine a student who consistently blames others when things go wrong in group projects. They take on the role of the victim, damaging their reputation as someone who doesn't take responsibility. Another student often steps in to "rescue" them, taking on the role of the caregiver/rescuer, and this dynamic prevents both students from growing or building trust. The reputation of the "rescuer" may suffer because others see them as someone who enables irresponsibility.

Breaking this cycle requires both students to take ownership of their actions. The victim must recognize their part in the situation, and the rescuer must step back and allow the other person to learn from their mistakes. By doing this, they build a reputation of responsibility and accountability.

Let's Make It Real:

Invite students to talk to the person next to them about a time when they found themselves or someone else stuck in the irresponsibility cycle. How did taking on the role of victim, rescuer, or bad guy affect their reputation or the relationship?

Discuss:

- How does taking on roles like the victim, rescuer, or bad guy affect how others see us?
- Can you think of a time when breaking the irresponsibility cycle helped you or someone else build a more positive reputation?
- What are some ways you can avoid falling into the irresponsibility cycle in your relationships?

Connect:

- How do you think you're going with this skill in your own life?
- If you had to give yourself a score out of 10 (10 being awesome), what would you give yourself?
- Can you think of someone who's really good at this? What do they do that stands out to you?
- What's one small thing you can try this week to bump your score up by one point?

Do:

This week, focus on breaking the irresponsibility cycle in your relationships. Take ownership of your actions and avoid blaming others, rescuing, or taking on unnecessary blame. Reflect on how taking responsibility helps you build a stronger, more positive reputation.

End-of-Week Reflection:

At the end of the week, ask yourself:

- How did I take ownership of my actions this week?
- What situations allowed me to break the irresponsibility cycle and take responsibility?
- What have I learned about building a positive reputation through accountability?

WEEK 27:

BECOMING A POWERFUL PERSON

"Powerful people take responsibility for their lives and choices. Powerful people choose who they want to be with, what they are going to pursue in life, and how they are going to go after it."
—Danny Silk

Learn:

Becoming a powerful person means taking responsibility for yourself and how you interact with others. Powerful people set limits and boundaries because they know their value and respect both themselves and others. They understand that respectful relationships are built on mutual trust, and they are responsible for managing their own behaviour, regardless of what others are doing.

Being powerful doesn't mean controlling others—it means controlling yourself. A powerful person knows their worth and sets boundaries to protect their well-being. They expect respect from others because they treat themselves and others with respect. They don't let other people's actions determine how they feel or behave. Instead, they manage themselves and choose how to respond in every situation, even when faced with challenges or disrespect.

Powerful people:

1. **Require Respectful Relationships**: They demand respect from themselves and others, not by controlling others, but by consistently respecting themselves.

2. **Set Limits and Boundaries**: They know their value and set healthy boundaries to protect their mental and emotional health.

3. **Manage Themselves**: No matter what others are doing, powerful people remain responsible for their own actions, emotions, and choices. They don't let others dictate how they respond.

Consider:

Imagine a student who is being teased by a classmate. Instead of retaliating or letting the other person's actions dictate their behaviour, the student takes a powerful approach. They calmly set a boundary by saying, "I don't appreciate being treated this way, and I expect respect." The student walks away from the situation, showing that they are responsible for managing themselves, regardless of the classmate's behaviour. This shows self-respect and personal power.

Let's Make It Real:

Invite students to talk to the person next to them about a time when they set a boundary or stood up for themselves in a respectful way.

How did setting limits or managing themselves help them feel more powerful in the situation?

Discuss:

- What does it mean to be a powerful person, and how is that different from trying to control others?
- Can you think of a time when setting a boundary helped you protect yourself or a relationship?
- How can managing yourself, regardless of what others are doing, help you build more respectful relationships?

Connect:

- How do you think you're going with this skill in your own life?
- If you had to give yourself a score out of 10 (10 being awesome), what would you give yourself?
- Can you think of someone who's really good at this? What do they do that stands out to you?
- What's one small thing you can try this week to bump your score up by one point?

Do:

This week, focus on becoming a powerful person. Practice setting healthy boundaries and managing yourself, even when others aren't acting respectfully. Reflect on how taking control of your actions and emotions helps you feel more empowered and build stronger relationships.

End-of-Week Reflection:

At the end of the week, ask yourself:

- How did I take ownership of my actions this week?
- What situations allowed me to practice becoming a powerful person?
- What have I learned about setting boundaries and managing myself that I can apply moving forward?

WEEK 28:

RESTORING SELF-RESPECT

"I cannot conceive of a greater loss than the loss of one's self-respect."
—Mahatma Gandhi

Learn:

Self-respect means valuing yourself and treating yourself with kindness, care, and dignity. It's about recognising your worth and making choices that honour who you are. When we make mistakes or feel down, it can be easy to lose sight of our self-respect, but it's important to remember that everyone deserves to be treated with respect, including yourself. Restoring self-respect involves forgiving yourself, learning from your mistakes, and making decisions that support your growth and happiness.

Consider:

A student struggles with a difficult assignment and feels bad about not doing well. Instead of giving up or being hard on themselves, they take responsibility, ask for help, and improve on the next assignment. By making choices that support their growth, they restore their confidence and self-respect.

Let's Make It Real:

Invite students to talk to the person next to them about a time when they felt they had to restore their self-respect after a mistake or challenge. How did they go about doing it, and what helped them regain confidence?

Discuss:

- Why is self-respect important for personal growth and happiness?
- Can you think of a time when you needed to restore your self-respect? What steps did you take?
- What can you do each day to treat yourself with respect, especially during difficult times?

Connect:

- How do you think you're going with this skill in your own life?
- If you had to give yourself a score out of 10 (10 being awesome), what would you give yourself?
- Can you think of someone who's really good at this? What do they do that stands out to you?
- What's one small thing you can try this week to bump your score up by one point?

Do:

This week, focus on treating yourself with respect. If you make a mistake or face a challenge, forgive yourself and take steps to learn and grow from the experience. Notice how restoring self-respect helps you feel more confident and positive.

End-of-Week Reflection:

- How did you practice self-respect this week, especially after a challenge or mistake?
- Were there moments where restoring self-respect helped you feel more confident?
- What did you learn about treating yourself with respect during difficult times?

WEEK 29:

TAKING INITIATIVE WITH THE EMPOWERMENT MODEL

"Action cures fear."
—Mel Robbins

Learn:

The Empowerment Model is a way of guiding people to solve problems and take control of their actions, and it includes six key steps:

1. **Empathy**: This is about acknowledging when something goes wrong. For example, saying, "Oh no, that's tough!" shows that you understand the challenge.

2. **Empower**: Instead of fixing the problem for someone, ask, "What are you going to do?" This helps the person realise they have the power to make decisions.

3. **Explore**: Ask, "What have you tried?" to get them to think about what actions they've already taken.

4. **Educate**: If they need help, you can say, "I have some ideas if you'd like to hear them," but you're not telling them what to do—you're offering guidance.

5. **Expect**: Ask, "What will you do now?" This is where the person takes ownership of their next step.

6. **Encourage**: Finally, say, "Let me know how you go." This encourages them to follow through and keeps the conversation open for future reflection.

Taking initiative is a great example of the Empowerment Model in action. When you take initiative, you're moving through these steps yourself—recognising a problem, thinking through solutions, and taking action. Empowered individuals understand that they have the power to make decisions and influence the outcome, rather than waiting for someone else to step in.

Consider:

During a group project, one student notices that the team is struggling to prioritise tasks, with some focusing on less important things. Instead of waiting for someone else to take charge, this student decides to take initiative and walks through the Empowerment Model.

- First, they show **Empathy**: "Oh no, it looks like we're a bit behind on what's most important."

- Then, they **Empower** their teammates: "What are we going to do to get back on track?"

- Next, they **Explore**: "What have we already tried to fix this?"

- They offer **Education**: "I have some ideas if you'd like to hear them."

- After a plan is discussed, they set an **Expectation**: "What will we do now?"

- Finally, they **Encourage** the team: "Let's check in tomorrow and see how we're doing."

By following these steps, the student is empowered and helps empower their team to take control of the situation and move forward effectively.

Let's Make It Real:

Invite students to talk to the person next to them about a time when they saw a problem and could have used the Empowerment Model. How could they have applied each step to take initiative and guide the situation toward a solution?

Discuss:

- How does the Empowerment Model help you feel more in control when facing a problem?

- Can you think of a time when taking initiative helped solve a problem or improve a situation?

- How could using the Empowerment Model help you in group projects, at home, or in other areas of life?

Connect:

- How do you think you're going with this skill in your own life?

- If you had to give yourself a score out of 10 (10 being awesome), what would you give yourself?

- Can you think of someone who's really good at this? What do they do that stands out to you?

- What's one small thing you can try this week to bump your score up by one point?

Do:

This week, look for a chance to use the Empowerment Model. Whether it's in a group project, solving a problem, or helping someone else, walk through each step: Empathy, Empower, Explore, Educate, Expect, and Encourage. Notice how following this process helps you and others feel more in control and confident.

End-of-Week Reflection:

At the end of the week, ask yourself:

- When did I see a problem this week and decide to step up instead of waiting for someone else?
- Which parts of the Empowerment Model did I use, and how did it help?
- How did taking initiative make things better for me and for others?

WEEK 30:

BEING A ROLE MODEL

"If you want to bring happiness to the whole world,
go home and love your family."
—Mother Teresa

Learn:

A role model is someone who leads by example and inspires others through their actions and behaviour. Being a role model means consistently doing what's right, even when it's difficult. It's not about being perfect, but about making good choices, treating others with respect, and showing responsibility. People look up to role models because they set a positive example that others want to follow. Whether you realise it or not, your actions can influence those around you, so being a role model is a powerful way to make a positive impact.

Consider:

A student is known for always helping classmates, staying focused during lessons, and being respectful to teachers. Without even knowing it, their behaviour inspires others to do the same. By being a role model, they create a positive environment and encourage others to follow their lead.

Let's Make It Real:

Invite students to talk to the person next to them about a role model they admire. What actions or qualities make that person someone they look up to? How can they be a role model for others?

Discuss:

- Why is it important to be a role model, especially for younger students or peers?
- Can you think of a time when someone's positive example inspired you to do better?
- What actions or behaviours can you practice to become a role model for others?

Connect:

- How do you think you're going with this skill in your own life?
- If you had to give yourself a score out of 10 (10 being awesome), what would you give yourself?
- Can you think of someone who's really good at this? What do they do that stands out to you?

- What's one small thing you can try this week to bump your score up by one point?

Do:

This week, focus on being a role model through your actions. Whether it's by showing kindness, responsibility, or leadership, notice how your behaviour influences others and creates a positive impact.

End-of-Week Reflection:

- How did you act as a role model this week, and who might have been influenced by your actions?
- Were there any moments where your behaviour set a positive example for others?
- What did you learn about the responsibility of being a role model?

PART FOUR

EMPOWERING STUDENT LEADERSHIP

Being a leader isn't just about being in charge—it's about showing others what's possible by the way you carry yourself.

In this section, students will discover what leadership really means in everyday life—whether it's in the classroom, with friends, or at home. They'll learn how to manage their own choices, set healthy boundaries, lift others up, and make decisions that line up with their values.

Together, we'll explore what it looks like to lead with empathy, courage, and integrity. This isn't about having all the answers—it's about being someone others can trust, someone who takes initiative, and someone who helps build a community where everyone feels seen, safe, and supported.

WEEK 31:

SERVICE TO OTHERS

*"The measure of a leader is not the number of people who
serve him but the number of people he serves."*
—John C. Maxwell

Learn:

Service to others means helping people without expecting anything in
return. It's about giving your time, energy, or skills to make someone
else's life better. Acts of service create a sense of community, build empathy, and help us develop a deeper connection with those around us.
Whether it's helping a classmate with their work, volunteering, or simply
being kind, serving others allows us to grow and make a positive impact.

Consider:

During recess, one student notices a classmate struggling to carry their
books. Instead of just watching, they step in to help. Though it's a small

act of service, the gesture makes the classmate's day easier and strengthens their connection. By serving others, the student builds a reputation for kindness and reliability.

Let's Make It Real:

Invite students to talk to the person next to them about a time when they helped someone or were helped by someone else. How did that act of service make them feel, and what impact did it have?

Discuss:

- Why is it important to help others, even when you don't get anything in return?
- Can you think of a time when an act of service made a difference in your life or someone else's?
- What are some ways you can serve others in your school, home, or community?

Connect:

- How do you think you're going with this skill in your own life?
- If you had to give yourself a score out of 10 (10 being awesome), what would you give yourself?
- Can you think of someone who's really good at this? What do they do that stands out to you?
- What's one small thing you can try this week to bump your score up by one point?

Do:

This week, focus on finding ways to serve others—whether it's helping a friend, classmate, or family member. Notice how acts of service help build stronger connections and make a positive difference.

End-of-Week Reflection:

- How did you serve others this week, and how did it make you feel?

- Were there any moments where your act of service made a positive difference for someone else?

- What did you learn about the importance of helping others without expecting anything in return?

WEEK 32:

MENTORING PEERS

"You MATTER."
—John Griffen (my mentor)

Learn:

Mentoring peers means offering support, guidance, and encouragement to help someone grow and succeed. Mentors share their knowledge and experiences to help others overcome challenges and reach their goals. You don't have to be older or more experienced to be a mentor—sometimes, just being there to listen and offer advice can make a big difference in someone's life. Being a mentor helps you develop leadership skills while building strong, positive relationships.

Consider:

One student notices a classmate struggling with their homework. Instead of just offering a quick answer, they take the time to explain the problem and guide their classmate through the process. By acting as a mentor, the student helps their peer build confidence and develop the skills they need to succeed. Both students benefit from the experience—the mentor strengthens their own understanding and the peer gains valuable support.

Let's Make It Real:

Invite students to talk to the person next to them about a time when they helped mentor someone or were mentored by a peer. How did this support help them or their classmate succeed?

Discuss:

- Why is it important to mentor others and share what you know?
- Can you think of a time when someone's guidance or support helped you through a challenge?
- What are some ways you can be a mentor to someone in your classroom or community?

Connect:

- How do you think you're going with this skill in your own life?
- If you had to give yourself a score out of 10 (10 being awesome), what would you give yourself?
- Can you think of someone who's really good at this? What do they do that stands out to you?
- What's one small thing you can try this week to bump your score up by one point?

Do:

This week, look for opportunities to mentor a peer. Offer support, guidance, or advice to someone who needs help. Notice how being a mentor strengthens your own skills and helps others grow.

End-of-Week Reflection:

- How did you mentor or support a peer this week, and what impact did it have?
- Did you feel more confident or connected through helping someone else?
- What did you learn about the value of mentoring others?

WEEK 33:

PRIORITISE SUCCESS

"You Are One Decision Away from a Completely Different Life!"
—Mel Robbins

Learn:

Priority management is about deciding what tasks are most important and focusing on those first. Stephen Covey says it this way: "The key is not to prioritise what's on your schedule, but to schedule your priorities." We all have limited time in a day, but how we use that time depends on what we prioritise. By managing priorities well, we can complete the most important tasks efficiently, reduce stress, and create time for the things that matter most. Learning to prioritise tasks, avoid distractions, and focus on what's important can lead to more success in school and life.

Consider:

In class, one student makes a list of the most important homework tasks and focuses on completing those first, while another student spends time on less important activities and leaves their homework until last. The student who prioritises well finishes their important tasks and feels accomplished, while the other student feels stressed because they didn't manage their priorities effectively.

Let's Make It Real:

Invite students to talk to the person next to them about a time when prioritising tasks helped them succeed or when focusing on the wrong things caused stress. What did they learn from the experience?

Discuss:

- Why is it important to prioritise tasks in both school and personal life?
- Can you think of a time when you felt stressed because you didn't focus on what was most important?
- What is one thing you can do this week to manage your priorities better?

Connect:

- How do you think you're going with this skill in your own life?
- If you had to give yourself a score out of 10 (10 being awesome), what would you give yourself?
- Can you think of someone who's really good at this? What do they do that stands out to you?

- What's one small thing you can try this week to bump your score up by one point?

Do:

This week, make a list of your tasks and identify the most important ones. Focus on completing those first before moving on to other activities. Notice how managing your priorities helps you feel more in control and less stressed.

End-of-Week Reflection:

- How did you manage your priorities this week?
- Did focusing on what was most important help you accomplish more?
- What did you learn about balancing your tasks and responsibilities?

WEEK 34:

PROBLEM-SOLVING SKILLS

"We cannot solve our problems with the same level
of thinking that created them."
—ALBERT EINSTEIN

Learn:

Problem-solving skills are essential for tackling challenges, both big and small. It's about thinking critically, staying calm, and working through problems step by step to find solutions. Problem-solving often involves creativity and persistence, as well as the ability to listen to others' ideas and collaborate when needed. Developing strong problem-solving skills helps us feel more confident in overcoming obstacles and leads to better outcomes in both school and life.

Consider:

During a group project, the team encounters a problem when their initial plan doesn't work as expected. Instead of getting frustrated or giving up, one student suggests brainstorming alternative solutions. The group works together to come up with new ideas and tests them out until they find one that works. By using their problem-solving skills, the team successfully overcomes the challenge and finishes the project.

Let's Make It Real:

Invite students to talk to the person next to them about a time when they had to solve a problem. How did they approach the situation, and what steps did they take to find a solution?

Discuss:

- Why is it important to stay calm and think critically when facing a problem?
- Can you think of a time when a creative solution helped you solve a challenge?
- What strategies can you use to improve your problem-solving skills in the classroom or in daily life?

Connect:

- How do you think you're going with this skill in your own life?
- If you had to give yourself a score out of 10 (10 being awesome), what would you give yourself?
- Can you think of someone who's really good at this? What do they do that stands out to you?
- What's one small thing you can try this week to bump your score up by one point?

Do:

This week, if you face a challenge or problem, focus on staying calm and thinking critically. Break the problem down into smaller steps, consider different solutions, and ask for help if needed. Reflect on how your problem-solving skills helped you overcome the challenge.

End-of-Week Reflection:

- What problems did you solve this week, and how did you approach them?
- Were there moments where your problem-solving skills helped you or your group succeed?
- What did you learn about thinking critically and creatively to solve challenges?

WEEK 35:

EMPOWERING CHOICES

*"You are free to choose, but you are not free to alter
the consequences of your decisions."*
— Ezra Taft Benson

Learn:

Powerful individuals understand that they have the ability to make their own choices and take responsibility for the consequences. They recognise that their decisions can shape their future, and they act with intention. On the other hand, powerless individuals may feel as though choices are made for them or that they have no control over the outcome. Empowering choices come from understanding the power you have over your own actions and realising that even small decisions can have a big impact.

Consider:

One student is faced with the choice of studying for an upcoming test or playing video games. By acting powerfully, they decide to study first, knowing that this choice will help them feel more prepared and relaxed afterward. A powerless choice would have been to give in to distractions and then blame the lack of time for poor performance on the test.

Let's Make It Real:

Invite students to talk to the person next to them about a time when they made an empowered, powerful choice. How did that decision make them feel more in control? Discuss a time when they made a powerless choice and how it affected the outcome.

Discuss:

- Why is it important to think about the consequences of your choices before acting?
- Can you think of a time when making an empowered choice led to a positive outcome?
- What are some ways you can make empowered choices in school, at home, or with friends?

Connect:

- How do you think you're going with this skill in your own life?
- If you had to give yourself a score out of 10 (10 being awesome), what would you give yourself?
- Can you think of someone who's really good at this? What do they do that stands out to you?

- What's one small thing you can try this week to bump your score up by one point?

Do:

This week, focus on making powerful choices. Take time to think through your decisions and recognise the power you have in shaping your outcomes. Reflect on how making intentional, empowered choices helps you feel more responsible and in control.

End-of-Week Reflection:

At the end of the week, ask yourself:

- What's one powerful choice I made this week, and how did it affect the outcome?
- Did I notice any powerless choices I made? What were the consequences?
- How can I practise making more empowered choices next week?

WEEK 36:

HEALTHY BOUNDARIES
IN LEADERSHIP

"Boundaries are to protect life, to protect love, to protect freedom."
—Henry Cloud

Learn:

Healthy boundaries in leadership are about understanding your limits and respecting the limits of others. Whether in friendships, school, or group activities, setting boundaries helps maintain respect and prevents burnout. Good leaders know when to say "no," when to ask for help, and how to create an environment where everyone feels valued and respected. By establishing healthy boundaries, you can lead effectively while also taking care of yourself and others.

Consider:

A student who leads a group project notices that they are taking on too much of the work. Instead of feeling overwhelmed, they set a boundary by asking their teammates to share more of the responsibilities. By communicating their needs clearly, they create a more balanced and fair work environment where everyone contributes, and the project is completed successfully. Setting this boundary also prevents the student from feeling stressed or burned out.

Let's Make It Real:

Invite students to talk to the person next to them about a time when they set a boundary or saw someone else set a boundary in a leadership role. How did setting this boundary help improve the situation?

Discuss:

- Why are healthy boundaries important for effective leadership and teamwork?
- Can you think of a time when setting a boundary helped you or someone else avoid burnout or stress?
- What are some boundaries you can set to ensure balance in your responsibilities at school or in friendships?

Connect:

- How do you think you're going with this skill in your own life?
- If you had to give yourself a score out of 10 (10 being awesome), what would you give yourself?
- Can you think of someone who's really good at this? What do they do that stands out to you?
- What's one small thing you can try this week to bump your score up by one point?

Do:

This week, focus on setting healthy boundaries in your leadership or group roles. Communicate your limits clearly, and make sure to respect the boundaries of others. Notice how setting boundaries helps create a more positive and balanced environment for everyone.

End-of-Week Reflection:

- How did setting or respecting boundaries help you this week, especially in leadership roles?
- Were there any moments where boundaries improved a group project or relationship?
- What did you learn about the importance of setting healthy boundaries in leadership?

WEEK 37:

CELEBRATING SUCCESSES TOGETHER

"Success is best when it's shared."
—HOWARD SCHULTZ

Learn:

Celebrating successes together means recognising and appreciating the achievements of others, as well as your own. Whether big or small, celebrating successes as a group helps build a sense of community and encourages everyone to keep striving for their goals. When we take the time to acknowledge our hard work and the accomplishments of others, we create a positive environment where success is shared and appreciated.

Consider:

A class completes a challenging project, and their teacher takes time to highlight everyone's contributions. Each student feels proud of what they've accomplished, and the group takes a moment to celebrate their hard work. By celebrating together, the students feel more connected and motivated to keep working toward future successes.

Let's Make It Real:

Invite students to talk to the person next to them about a time when they celebrated a success with others. How did sharing that moment with a group make the success feel even more meaningful?

Discuss:

- Why is it important to celebrate successes, both your own and others'?
- Can you think of a time when celebrating with others made an achievement feel even better?
- How can you encourage a culture of celebration and recognition in your classroom or group?

Connect:

- How do you think you're going with this skill in your own life?
- If you had to give yourself a score out of 10 (10 being awesome), what would you give yourself?
- Can you think of someone who's really good at this? What do they do that stands out to you?
- What's one small thing you can try this week to bump your score up by one point?

Do:

This week, take time to celebrate the successes of others as well as your own. Whether it's completing a project, reaching a goal, or helping someone else, share your achievements and recognise the hard work of those around you. Notice how celebrating together builds a stronger, more positive community.

End-of-Week Reflection:

- How did you celebrate successes with your classmates or friends this week?

- Did celebrating with others make the achievement feel more meaningful?

- What did you learn about the importance of recognising group success?

WEEK 38:

ENCOURAGING GROWTH IN OTHERS

"The greatest leader is not necessarily the one who does the greatest things. They are the one that gets people to do the greatest things."
—Ronald Reagan

Learn:

Encouraging growth in others means supporting and motivating them to reach their potential. It's about recognising the strengths and abilities of your peers and helping them improve. By offering guidance, positive feedback, and encouragement, you help others develop confidence and skills. When we focus on helping others grow, we create a culture of support where everyone feels valued and motivated to do their best.

Consider:

A student notices that their classmate is hesitant to answer a question in class. Instead of letting them stay quiet, the student offers encouragement, saying, "I think you know the answer, go for it!" The classmate answers the question confidently and feels more comfortable participating in the future. By encouraging growth, the student helps their peer gain confidence and improve their classroom engagement.

Let's Make It Real:

Invite students to talk to the person next to them about a time when someone encouraged them to grow or when they encouraged someone else. How did that encouragement help them improve or take on a new challenge?

Discuss:

- Why is it important to encourage growth in others, especially in a group or classroom setting?
- Can you think of a time when someone's encouragement helped you step out of your comfort zone and grow?
- What are some ways you can support and encourage the growth of others in your classroom or community?

Connect:

- How do you think you're going with this skill in your own life?
- If you had to give yourself a score out of 10 (10 being awesome), what would you give yourself?
- Can you think of someone who's really good at this? What do they do that stands out to you?
- What's one small thing you can try this week to bump your score up by one point?

Do:

This week, focus on encouraging the growth of someone around you. Offer positive feedback, support, or advice to help them improve or take on a new challenge. Notice how your encouragement helps them feel more confident and motivated to succeed.

End-of-Week Reflection:

- How did you encourage the growth of others this week?
- Were there any moments when supporting someone helped them achieve more?
- What did you learn about the role of encouragement in helping others grow?

WEEK 39:

HANDLING DISAPPOINTMENT

"I've missed more than 9,000 shots in my career.
I've lost almost 300 games. Twenty-six times, I've been trusted to
take the game-winning shot and missed. I've failed over and over
and over again in my life. And that is why I succeed."
—MICHAEL JORDAN

Learn:

Handling disappointment is about learning how to cope with setbacks and challenges in a positive way. Disappointments are inevitable in life, whether it's missing out on something you wanted or not achieving a goal. Instead of letting disappointment bring you down, it's important to reflect, learn from the experience, and move forward with a stronger mindset. Resilience in the face of disappointment helps you grow and prepares you for future successes.

Consider:

A student works hard on a project but doesn't receive the grade they were hoping for. Instead of feeling discouraged and giving up, they talk to their teacher, learn what they can improve, and commit to doing better next time. By handling their disappointment with a positive attitude, the student learns valuable lessons and becomes more resilient in the face of future challenges.

Let's Make It Real:

Invite students to talk to the person next to them about a time when they faced disappointment. How did they handle the situation, and what did they learn from the experience?

Discuss:

- Why is it important to handle disappointment in a positive way rather than letting it bring you down?
- Can you think of a time when handling disappointment helped you learn or grow?
- What are some strategies you can use to deal with disappointment in school or life?

Connect:

- How do you think you're going with this skill in your own life?
- If you had to give yourself a score out of 10 (10 being awesome), what would you give yourself?

- Can you think of someone who's really good at this? What do they do that stands out to you?

- What's one small thing you can try this week to bump your score up by one point?

Do:

This week, if you face a disappointment, focus on reflecting on what you can learn from the experience. Use it as an opportunity to grow and come back stronger. Notice how handling disappointment positively helps you build resilience and move forward.

End-of-Week Reflection:

- How did you handle disappointment this week, and what did you learn from it?

- Were there moments where turning disappointment into a learning experience helped you grow?

- What did you learn about resilience and moving forward after a setback?

WEEK 40:

CELEBRATING GROWTH

"Remember to celebrate milestones as you prepare for the road ahead."
—Nelson Mandela

Learn:

Celebrating growth means recognising the progress you've made—big or small—and appreciating how far you've come. Growth isn't just about ticking off a goal, it's also about the steps you've taken along the way. When you pause to celebrate your personal development, you build confidence and motivation to keep going. Whether it's academic progress, social skills, or emotional growth, every step forward matters—and celebrating helps remind you just how capable you really are.

Consider:

A student who used to struggle with public speaking now feels confident presenting in front of the class. They take a moment to reflect on their progress and feel proud of how far they've come. Their classmates celebrate their achievement with encouraging feedback, which not only boosts confidence but inspires everyone to keep growing. When we recognise growth, we inspire a culture of encouragement and possibility.

Let's Make It Real:

Invite students to turn to the person next to them and share one area where they've grown this year. What helped them get there? Why is it important to take a moment to celebrate that progress?

Discuss:

- Why is it important to celebrate growth, even if you haven't reached your final goal yet?
- Can you think of a time when celebrating your growth gave you the push to keep going?
- How can recognising growth in others help build a stronger classroom or school culture?

Connect:

In your *Connect Group*, reflect on each of the four areas we've explored this year. Take turns answering the same four questions for each:

Healthy Relationships
Joyful Responsibility
Genuine Restoration
Empowering Leadership

For each area, ask:

1. How do you think you're going with this in your own life?

2. If you had to give yourself a score out of 10 (10 being awesome), what would you give yourself?

3. Can you think of someone who's really good at this? What do they do that stands out to you?

4. What's one small thing you could try to bump your score up by one point?

Encourage honesty and encouragement within the group. This is a time to reflect, celebrate, and support one another.

Do:

This week, take time to reflect on your personal growth—whether it's something you've improved on in school, a new skill you've developed, or a challenge you've worked through. Share your progress with someone you trust and celebrate how far you've come. Notice how this builds your confidence and encourages you to keep growing.

End-of-Week Reflection:

- How did you celebrate your personal growth—or the growth of someone else—this week?

- Were there any moments where recognising progress helped you feel more motivated?

- What did you learn about the power of celebrating even small steps of growth?

BONUS TOPICS

Think of this Bonus Section as some extra goodness for those weeks when the term runs a little longer than usual!

These extra sessions are designed to build on everything students have already learned — giving them more chances to reflect, grow, and keep building their leadership muscles. Whether it's diving deeper into responsibility, strengthening relationships, or growing in personal confidence, these sessions offer fresh challenges and meaningful conversations to keep the momentum going.

It's all about continuing the journey and giving students more space to grow into the powerful, respectful, and connected people they're becoming.

BONUS:

CHOICES AND CONSEQUENCES

"Life is a matter of choices, and every choice you make makes you."
—JOHN C. MAXWELL

Learn:

Every choice we make, big or small, leads to a consequence. Some consequences are immediate, like getting a good grade after studying hard, and others may take time, like building trust through kind actions. Understanding that our choices shape our lives is an important step in learning responsibility. By making thoughtful decisions, we can create positive outcomes for ourselves and those around us.

Consider:

In the classroom, a student decides to talk during a lesson. As a consequence, they miss out on important information and feel confused during the next task. Meanwhile, another student chooses to focus and complete their work, leading to a sense of accomplishment and praise from the teacher. Both students made choices, but the outcomes were very different.

Let's Make It Real:

Invite students to talk to the person next to them and share a time when a choice they made had a consequence—either positive or negative. How did that consequence affect them or others?

Discuss:

- Can you think of a choice you made recently and what the outcome was?
- Why is it important to think about the consequences before making a decision?
- How do positive choices lead to better results in your relationships or learning?

Connect:

- How do you think you're going with this skill in your own life?
- If you had to give yourself a score out of 10 (10 being awesome), what would you give yourself?
- Can you think of someone who's really good at this? What do they do that stands out to you?
- What's one small thing you can try this week to bump your score up by one point?

Do:

This week, before making a decision, pause and think about what the consequence of that choice might be. After making your decision, reflect on the outcome and how it affected you or others.

End-of-Week Reflection:

- What choices did you make this week, and how did they impact you or others?
- Were there any consequences that surprised you, either positive or negative?
- What did you learn about thinking through your choices before acting?

BONUS:

SETTING PERSONAL GOALS

"Setting goals is the first step in turning the invisible into the visible."
—Tony Robbins

Learn:

Setting personal goals helps us take control of our future by giving us direction and purpose. When we have clear goals, we know what we're working toward and can make plans to achieve them. Goals give us motivation and help us track our progress, whether we're aiming to improve in school, build stronger relationships, or develop new skills. By setting personal goals, we take responsibility for our growth and become more empowered to succeed.

Consider:

A student in class decides they want to improve their reading skills. They set a goal to read for 20 minutes each day. Over time, they notice their reading speed increases, and they feel more confident during class discussions. The small, consistent action of working toward their goal made a big difference in their skills and self-esteem.

Let's Make It Real:

Invite students to talk to the person next to them and share a goal they've set in the past or would like to set for the future. Discuss how they plan to achieve it and what steps they can take.

Discuss:

- Why is it important to set personal goals, and how do they help us stay focused?
- Can you think of a time when setting a goal helped you accomplish something important?
- What is one goal you can set for yourself that will help you grow in school or life?

Connect:

- How do you think you're going with this skill in your own life?
- If you had to give yourself a score out of 10 (10 being awesome), what would you give yourself?
- Can you think of someone who's really good at this? What do they do that stands out to you?
- What's one small thing you can try this week to bump your score up by one point?

Do:

This week, set a personal goal for yourself—whether it's related to your schoolwork, friendships, or a new skill. Write it down and share it with the class or a friend. Track your progress and celebrate when you achieve it!

End-of-Week Reflection:

- Did you set a personal goal this week? How did you work toward it?
- What challenges did you face, and how did setting a goal help you overcome them?
- What did you learn about the importance of setting goals for yourself?

BONUS:

INCLUSION AND DIVERSITY

"I can do things you cannot, you can do things I cannot:
together we can do great things."
—MOTHER TERESA

Learn:

Inclusion means making sure that everyone feels welcome and valued, no matter who they are or where they come from. Diversity is about recognising and celebrating our differences, whether it's our background, culture, interests, or abilities. By embracing diversity, we learn from each other and grow as individuals. When we make an effort to include others and appreciate what makes them unique, we create a more accepting and respectful environment.

Consider:

During a group activity, a student notices that one of their classmates is often left out because they are shy. Instead of ignoring it, the student invites their classmate to join in, making them feel included and valued. By doing this, the student helps create a more inclusive and welcoming classroom for everyone.

Let's Make It Real:

Invite students to talk to the person next to them about a time when they were included in a group or when they made an effort to include someone else. How did this inclusion affect the experience for everyone?

Activity: The Continuum of Likes and Dislikes

Objective: This interactive activity will help students understand and appreciate diversity by showing how we all have different preferences, yet all of our opinions are valuable.

1. **Set the Scene:** Mark a line across the room or basketball court with "I Love" on one end and "I Don't Like" on the other.
2. **Instructions:** Explain that you will ask a series of questions, and for each question, students will stand somewhere on the line based on how much they like or dislike something:

   - If they really love something, they stand closer to the "I Love" side.
   - If they really don't like something, they stand closer to the "I Don't Like" side.
   - If they're unsure, they can stand somewhere in the middle.

3. **Ask Questions:** Example questions to ask the students:

- "How do you feel about getting your driver's licence?"
- "Do you like cleaning your room?"
- "How do you feel about hanging out with your parents?"
- "Do you like playing sports?"
- "Do you enjoy the beach?"

Discuss:

- Why is it important to include others, especially those who may be different from us?
- Can you think of a time when diversity helped you learn something new or see things differently?
- How can you make an effort to include others in your classroom or activities?

Connect:

- How do you think you're going with this skill in your own life?
- If you had to give yourself a score out of 10 (10 being awesome), what would you give yourself?
- Can you think of someone who's really good at this? What do they do that stands out to you?
- What's one small thing you can try this week to bump your score up by one point?

Do:

This week, look for opportunities to include someone who may be left out or who is different from you. Show appreciation for their uniqueness and reflect on how inclusion creates a stronger and more positive environment.

End-of-Week Reflection:

- How did you include others this week, especially those who might feel left out?
- Were there any moments when you appreciated the diversity of your group?
- What did you learn about the importance of inclusion and valuing differences?

BONUS:

HANDLING PEER PRESSURE

"Be yourself; everyone else is already taken."
—Oscar Wilde

Learn:

Peer pressure happens when we feel pushed to do something because others are doing it or because we want to fit in. Sometimes, peer pressure can be positive, encouraging us to make good choices, but often it can lead us to do things we wouldn't normally do. Handling peer pressure means having the confidence to make your own decisions, even when it's hard, and staying true to your values. It's about standing up for yourself and not letting others control your choices.

Consider:

A group of students tries to convince one of their classmates to skip class with them. Even though the student feels tempted to go along with them, they decide to do the right thing and stay in class. By standing up to peer pressure, they stay true to their values and avoid getting into trouble. This choice earns them respect from others who admire their confidence.

Let's Make It Real:

Invite students to talk to the person next to them about a time when they faced peer pressure. How did they handle the situation, and what did they learn from it?

Discuss:

- Why is it important to resist peer pressure and make your own choices?
- Can you think of a time when peer pressure led to a positive or negative outcome?
- What strategies can you use to handle peer pressure in difficult situations?

Connect:

- How do you think you're going with this skill in your own life?
- If you had to give yourself a score out of 10 (10 being awesome), what would you give yourself?
- Can you think of someone who's really good at this? What do they do that stands out to you?
- What's one small thing you can try this week to bump your score up by one point?

Do:

This week, if you face peer pressure, remember to make your own choices and stay true to your values. Notice how making decisions for yourself helps you feel more confident and in control of your life.

End-of-Week Reflection:
- How did you handle peer pressure this week?
- Were there any situations where you stood up for your own values and made your own decisions?
- What did you learn about resisting peer pressure and staying true to yourself?

EQUIPPING A CULTURE OF LOVE

At Godwin Consulting, we believe in empowering educators and leaders to create environments where joy, responsibility and connection thrive. That's why we've designed a variety of resources to support you on your journey—whether you're working with students, staff, or leaders.

If you're looking to bring lasting change to your school, our LoSoP Foundations Course (online, self-paced) and LoSoP School Representative Programs (facilitated) offer tailored, in-depth training to guide you every step of the way. Whether you're looking to lead with joy and responsibility or turn your classroom into a space of growth and respect, we've got the tools, knowledge, and support to make it happen.

Our resources are all about making your day easier and more impactful. From practical classroom tools like our LoSoP Desk Flip and Diagram or Language Flashcards to our empowering Umbrella of Grace, each item is designed to bring connection and grace to your everyday teaching. We also have printable posters to help you keep the LoSoP philosophy front and centre in your work, plus online courses that dig deeper into the LoSoP principles and give you practical, actionable strategies.

Explore our website and find the resources that can make a difference in your school culture today. We're here to support you on your mission to nurture stronger, more connected communities.

Check out our online store at **www.godwinconsulting.com.au**

ABOUT THE AUTHOR

Bernii Godwin holds a Master's qualification in Social Work and a Graduate Certificate in Neuropsychotherapy, building on her undergraduate degree in Human Services and Criminology and Criminal Justice, with a focus on youth and family justice. She is also a certified Loving on Purpose Trainer and John Maxwell Leadership Team Member.

Over the past two decades, Bernii has worked in various roles across a wide range of schools, specializing in student well-being and behaviour. Principals frequently seek her expertise to consult on complex behaviour and well-being issues, provide one-on-one coaching or supervision to educators and well-being teams, and deliver school-wide professional development. Her greatest passion is helping schools adopt practical tools that replace fear and punishment with purposeful behaviour education, safe connections, and empowered teachers—ultimately increasing student engagement in their academic journey.

To connect with Bernii, please visit
www.godwinconsulting.com.au